Uncle Homer's Outdoor Chuckle Book

A Rare Catch of Folksy Jokes, Quips, Cartoons, and Keeper Memories

by Homer Circle

Angling Editor, Sports Afield

by Larsen's Outdoor Publishing

ISBN 0-936513-37-3

Library of Congress 93-79797

Published by

LARSEN'S OUTDOOR PUBLISHING
2640 Elizabeth Place
Lakeland, FL 33813
(813)644-3381

PRINTED IN THE UNITED STATES OF AMERICA

1 2 3 4 5 6 7 8 9 10

DEDICATION

Dedicated to my beloved wife, Gayle, who after 57 cherished years still is my "Childbride." If, in truth, I have "soared with the eagles" in my profession, then, beyond doubt, she has been the wind beneath my wings.

With special thanks to Jim Matlock, talented cartoonist and a genuinely nice guy, with a wife, Sue, to match!

FOREWORD

The impulse to write "Uncle Homer's Chuckle Book" came one night while meditating before a flickering camp fire. My thoughts conjured a montage of 50-plus years traipsing around the world...fishing, hunting, and writing about it in the company of unique outdoor characters.

I have been privileged to share moments with so many colorful companions, including fishing and hunting buddies, guides, conservation agents, executives, editors, governors, congressmen, a president, and especially native fishermen with idiomatic quips and yarns to spin.

Over all those years when I heard a "keeper tidbit" I followed an inner voice urging to write it down. I built a file fast as a pre-hibernation groundhog. Other chuckles came from a style I followed in writing outdoor columns for local newspapers wherever we lived in Ohio, Michigan, Arkansas and Florida, over several decades. I wound up each Sunday's department with several "smiles"...usually native humor.

Additionally, I have interspersed "keeper memories"...moments, happenings, thoughts that are moving, inspirational, humorous and worthy of sharing. Some have nothing to do with the outdoors but are included simply to lighten your moments.

Some of the classic yarns are missing because they are raunchy or downright dirty and not worthy of note. Some I have been able to "launder" to a degree of naughtiness but, I trust, not offensive. Many came when the hunting and fishing were so bad the redeeming feature was swapping campfire yarns, one punchline triggering another.

I look upon this chuckle book as a "load lightener" to give to an outdoorsy friend who is shut in, or not able to pursue favorite outdoor sports because of physical limitations. It is bound to create an afterglow of fond memories and lift spirits.

It is a sharing, and I urge you to help preserve our grand outdoors traditions by sharing them with others, both elderfolk and kids. As I have written: "Teach kids to hunt and fish...and they never will really grow old. That's because the kid in those who hunt and fish...never really grows up!"

ABOUT THE AUTHOR

"Uncle Homer" Circle figures he is the world's luckiest guy because he gets paid to fish and write about it. He has been Sports Afield Magazine's angling editor for 26 years and has covered four continents and 50 United States in quest of article material.

He holds four world records, set in 1992, and has spent a lifetime in this sport. He is past president of the Outdoor Writers Association of America, once Arkansas game and fish commissioner, has hosted three national TV shows, written seven books and starred in over 50 fishing films.

He also teaches fishing seminars to pass along the lore of his favorite sport, highlighting his lectures with a limit of outdoor tales collected from over half a century of selecting and filing the "keepers." This book contains the cream of the crop, touching myriad phases of his cherished outdoors.

Uncle Homer's
Outdoor Chuckle Book

● ● ● ● ● ● ● ● ● ● ● ● ● ● ● ● ●

CATFISH FISHERMEN have to be the raunchiest smelling of all because they use the stinkiest baits. Like leaving shrimp or liver to age on the back porch until the neighbors complain and the buzzards are circling outside.

This particular catfisherman arrived home with a baby skunk under his arm. "Marthy," he said to his wife, "this here little skunk was wanderin' along the road and I knew it would die without its mama, so I brought it home. Do you suppose you could find a way to feed it tonight?"

His wife smiled and replied: "Why yes, I could use our daughter's little doll bottle, should be about the right size." She warmed some milk and the little bottle worked beautifully. But she thought...I wonder if it's against the law to keep a baby skunk? So she phoned the game warden and asked him.

He replied: "No ma'm, that's a very nice thing you're doing, otherwise that little skunk probably would die. But it does raise a question. How will you keep it warm tonight without its mama?" She said: "Well, I'll just put it in bed between me and pa. That ought to keep it warm."

The game warden shot back, "But, m'am, what about the smell?" And she replied: "Well, heck, let that little skunk get used to it...the same as I had to!"

FOSTER BROOKS, the standup comedian who has made a career using a drunken delivery to tell jokes, is a good fisherman and a delight to be in camp with because his droll stories come one after another. Here's my pick of his repertoir.

This fisherman came home very late, had downed too many beers, so he just sneaked past his wife who was asleep on the davenport. He crawled into bed and shortly after she came into the bedroom and began disrobing, giving him an icy stare. She took off her blouse, then her brassiere, and he blurted out, in a drunken drawl: "Bee-yoo-ti-ful...Bee-YOOOO-ti-ful!"

She shot back: "And just what is so beautiful?" He replied: "You (hickup) are! (Burp) First you took off your (hickup) blowze...then your (burp) brazzeer..and your buzzooms dropped down and pulled allll the wrinkles out of your face!"

• • • • • • • • • • • • • • • •

WHEN THE SCHOOLBUS stopped to pick up Zekie, he was leaning against the mail box, sound asleep. The bus driver tooted to rouse him and said, as Zekie mounted the steps: "Hey, boy, what's up? You're usually wide-eyed and bushytailed?"

Zekie yawned and replied: "Well, Mister Jones, it was a very long night. First, pa and me went fishin' and caught way too many bullheads. We were up cleaning them until midnight. "We finally got to bed and got woke up by a loud ruckus in the henhouse. So, pa got Ol' Betsy his double barrel shotgun, popped in two shells, and I got the flashlight.

"We were in our nightgowns and slippers, so we sneaked up to the henhouse door. I opened the door, eased the flashlight beam inside as pa cocked both barrels and poked the shotgun inside the henhouse. At that very moment our big hound dog, Ol' Blue, reached up under pa's nightgown and cold-nosed him. Whoo-boy, we were up all night...cleanin' chickens!"

THIS PARTICULAR preacher loved to fish. He planned to do so during his vacation week. But the wind blew so hard each day, Monday through Saturday, he couldn't launch his boat.

Sunday morning came and just as he was loading fishing tackle into his car...the wind died! He grabbed his gear, got in the boat and headed for the middle of the lake.

Upstairs in heaven, St. Peter saw this and said to the Lord: "Look, Jesus, there's a man of the cloth going fishing on this Sabbath day. How shall I punish him?"

The Lord smiled and replied: "Let me handle this one, Pete...I know fishermen." He watched as the preacher put on his favorite lure, made a long cast, and got a terrific strike. He set the hook, and after a long battle he landed a 50-pound largemouth bass!

St. Peter gasped: "Lord, Lord, that bass is more than twice the present world record! Do you call that punishment?" The Lord smiled and replied: "Think, Pete...who can he tell?"

• • • • • • • • • • • • • • • • •

AFTER ONE DELIGHTFUL trip to Ireland in search of whopper pike, we came home with three "keeper" stories typical of that nation's wit.

The first occured at the Shannon Airport where I had an hour to kill. So, I wandered outside wearing my jacket with a big, leaping bass on the left chest. An Irishman wearing a shortbilled cap was sitting on a bench and I noticed him eyeball my jacket as I stopped to look around.

Suddenly he began making casting and reeling motions with his bare hands, cutting side glances at me. I knew it was some sort of a come-on, so I strolled over and asked: "Are you catching any?" He looked up, gave me a one-sided grin, and replied: "Bejazus, you're the first one!"

11

THE FIRST GUIDE I hired was named Freddie McBrien, a tweed-attired man in his mid fifties. He was delightful company, we caught some picture-worthy pike, and spent the evening having supper at his small but neat cottage.

We sat chatting while his wife busied about the kitchen tidying up. I asked: "Freddie, how many years have you been a fishing guide?" Freddie replied, "Therty years it's been, and I've enjoyed all except one. Y'see, me back began killin' me, it did. And the doctor said: 'Freddie, ye durn fool, it's that pullin' the boat into the water and pullin' it out that's wreckin' yer back. So, just stop it and you'll be alright.'

"So for one year I did no guidin' at all, and I was miserable, I was. Then, one night after a mug of stout, I got to thinkin'...the doc said I could no longer pull the boat into the water and pull it out. So, I began pushin' the boat into the water and pushin' it out...and bejabbers I been guidin' ever since!"

• • • • • • • • • • • • • • • • •

TWO HILLBILLY squirrel hunters were out at crack o' dawn, settled down across from a big den tree. One was a stutterer and the other had the shakes. The stutterer won the coin toss so he got to take the first shot with the rifle they shared. After a short wait a squirrel emerged from the den, ran halfway down the tree and hung by its hind legs. The stutterer took careful aim, fired, missed, and the squirrel dashed back into the den. "Yuh-yuh-your turn," said the stutterer, handing over the rifle to the shaker. After a while the squirrel scampered down the tree and hung upside down. The shaker aimed, and aimed, shaking the gun barrel like a quaking aspen. He fired, and the squirrel fell to the ground, dead. "I got him!" said the shaker.

And the stutterer replied: "Well, huh-huh-hell yes...why shouldn't you...you aimed at the whole duh-damn-duh-damn-damned tree!"

AS MIKE WAS heading out fishing, Hanna stopped him at the door and said: "I've still got this horrible pain in me back...what should I do?" And Mike replied: "Hanna, I'm not a doctor so I wouldn't be knowin'. Why not phone the doctor and hear what he says. I'll see you when I come home."

When he returned that evening, he looked at her and said: "My gawd, Hanna, you've got a black eye, a torn ear, and a tooth out. What in the world has happened to ye?"

And Hanna heatedly replied: "Well, I phoned the doctor and he said: 'Hanna, I can't guess at something like this. Please get a small bottle and bring me a specimen.' "So, I got a small bottle and got to thinkin', what's a specimen? So, I went across the street to call on that nosey Missus O'Flaherity who knows everything. Holding the bottle up in me hand, I asked: 'Missus O'Flaherity, what is a specimen?' Looking me square in the eye she said: 'Go pee in the bottle.' And I shot back: 'Go poop in yer hat! Then she snorted: 'Frigg ye!'... and the fight was on!"

• • • • • • • • • • • • • • • • •

A POACHER CAUGHT catching fish illegally was basking in jail. His wife wrote to say: "Here it is spring, the potatoes need planting, but I'm not strong enough to dig up the back yard. You always did the digging and I did the planting. What in Hades are we going to do for food this winter?"

The poacher wrote back: "I've got to warn you to keep our secret. Do not, repeat, do not ever tell anyone about the money we have buried in the back yard."

Several days later the poacher received this letter from his wife: "A gang of men dressed in striped suits came out here and dug up our whole back yard. They wouldn't tell me what for. What should I do?"

And the poacher wrote back: "Now, plant the potatoes!"

THIS CITY FELLER inherited a lot of money when his grandfather died, so he lived it up. He bought a gilt Cadillac, wore pink suits, and tried to do all the things affluent folks did. This led him into hang gliding. And he got good at it. So, he headed West for California where the elitist hang gliders held forth.

As he drove through the Ozarks hills in Arkansas, he noticed a friendly breeze and deemed it a good place and time to get in a practice session. He strapped on his hang glider and was soaring nicely, riding the currents. Down below a couple of oldtimers were hunting wild turkeys. Both were nearsighted and squinted up at the soarer above.

One said: "What'n'ell kinda big bird is that?"

"Dunno," replied the other, "but hunker down and don't move, I believe he's headed this way. Keep yer haid down and don't even belch." So they both laid low and the pink-suited hang glider soared nearer and nearer. Suddenly the one with the shotgun jumped up and fired both barrels.

"Didja git that big bird?" asked the poorer sighted of the two. "Well, I musta hit it purty hard 'cause I made it drop that pink-suited dude it was a-carryin'."

• • • • • • • • • • • • • • • • •

TWO VERY OLD fishing buddies were out for their weekly crappie-catching fling, and Pete made several comments to Joe without so much as a nod, smile, or response of any kind. So Pete shouted: "Hey, Joe, can you hear me?"

Joe looked up, eyebrows elevated, and hollered back: "Whatchoo say?" with his hand cupped over his ear, revealing a small object stuck in the opening.

Pete peered closely, frowned, and bellowed: "Why-n-ell do you have a suppository stuck in your ear, you silly ol' fool?" And Joe replied: "Hey, thanks pal, now I know where I put my hearing aid!"

14

TWO FISHING BUDDIES were in service together. They talked and longed to return home to fish below the big dam where a monster catfish lived. It had broken 100-pound nylon lines and together they schemed a sure-fire scheme which would land that monster and set a new world record.

After the war they put it all together. They had a jeep with a 1,000-pound parachute cord tied to the rear axle. A blacksmith friend forged for them a huge treble hook which they tied to the end of the parachute cord. They covered it with 25 pounds of bloody beef liver. One got into a row boat, carried the baited monster hook out into the big eddy, tossed it out and rowed back to shore. He told his buddy: "Now I'll watch the cord and you sit on ready. When he takes the bait and heads for home, I'll holler and you set the hook. All set? Okay!"

He eagle-eyed the cord, patiently watched it twitch a couple times, and sat there shaking his head, not yet. Suddenly, the coils of cord paid out rapidly and he shouted at his buddy: "NOW, NOW SET THE HOOK!" His buddy raced the engine, let out the clutch, and took off at the jeep's top speed. The parachute cord pulled taut like a giant bull fiddle string. The jeep's wheels skidded for a few seconds, then it roared into the night. Something had to give!

Did they get that giant catfish, you ask? Well, no...but they did get 78 pounds of its lower jaw! And both are legends in their own minds.

● ● ● ● ● ● ● ● ● ● ● ● ● ● ● ● ●

TWO FISHING BUDDIES were on an annual outing and one came down with a miserable flu bug. The other said: "I just heard of a new cure. Fill the tub with the hottest water you can stand. Soak in it and sip a glassful of hot whisky toddy. When the toddy is all gone, either you'll be cured or you'll be the happiest sick man in town!"

GRANPA SCRAGGS fished Mill Creek since he was a kid. He never failed to catch bass on his pet lures. As he aged he began riding a bicycle to his pet fishing hole, with a basket for toting his tackle, for more fishing and less hiking time. The farmer who owned the area leased it for cattle grazing. A huge bull dominated the herd and resented any intruders. But this didn't deter Granpa Scraggs; he figured he had rights of prior domain. So he kept right on fishing.

One afternoon a young college student was cruising the adjoining dirt road with his date when they heard a series of shouts. They stopped to look and saw ol' Granpa peddling like mad, beard flowing back over his shoulder, cap on backwards, and that big bull only a couple gallops behind. Ol' Granpa headed for the rail fence near the couple, hit it head on, and flew over the top. He landed in a heap, his fish and tackle flying in all directions.

The young couple dusted him off, retrieved his gear, pulled his bike away from the snorting, stomping bull, and tried to calm him. The young man said: "That was close, old timer, that big bull almost got you!" And Granpa Scraggs retorted: "Yep, he almost gits me each time I go fishin'."

• • • • • • • • • • • • • • • • • •

THERE ARE MANY viewpoints on fishermen, depending on to whom you talk. Some describe a fisherman as a jerk at one end of a pole waiting for a jerk at the other end. Others say it's a person who does nothing all day and does it real slow. In reality, fishing is a time-honored sport loved and hobbied by peasants and presidents alike. Someone even wrote a poem to describe its intrigue. It goes like this: Of all the loves since the beginning of time, even greater than a babe for its mother; is the tender, compassionate, enduring love...of one lousy fisherman for another. And if that bit of doggerel doesn't touch you, then you've haven't spent enough hours doing more fishing than catching!

MOTHER TO SON: "I see you're going fishing. Why don't you take your little sister along?"

Son: "She keeps eating the bait, that's why!"

THIS GROUP OF OLDTIMERS had been holding an annual fishing trip for a couple generations. Each year one or more would bring along a son or nephew to break him into fishing. And there was a ritual involved, each newcomer had to sleep with ol' Hezzy who snored like a chainsaw cutting through an osage log. So, they got very little sleep.

One year the newcomer was a sharp, young cadet who spent the night with ol' Hezzy and showed up for breakfast, alert and chipper. A puzzled oldster eyed him and said: "I know you slept with ol' Hezzy last night, but you seem mighty alert this morning. Have any trouble sleeping? The young man smiled and replied: "Nope. But I had heard about his loud snoring before I came. So when I crawled into bed, I leaned over, giggled and kissed him on his ear. Ol' Hezzy just sat up in bed and watched me all night!"

• • • • • • • • • • • • • • • • • •

A HILLBILLY FISHERMAN was trying his luck on a very frosty morning, and he began shaking like a leaf. But he had brought along a flask of moonshine just in case. So, he took a few sips and it chased the chills away. It also made him gay (oldtime meaning) so he began humming to himself, even did a little jig.

Then he looked in his minnow bucket and suddenly felt sorry for the minnows because all they had to drink was water. So he trickled a little moonshine into the bucket, and the minnows became very active. He grabbed a fat one, hooked it through the tail, pitched it out near a patch of weeds, and the bobber was immediately jerked out of sight. He set the hook, then fought long and hard to bring in a hefty bass weighing about ten pounds. The minnow had the bass by the throat!

KEEPER MEMORY: I was fishing in Sweden on the Moorum River with Lenny Borgstrom, then president of ABU, makers of the unique Ambassadeur casting reel. Their camp was set up with a series of casting platforms to fly fish for Atlantic salmon and sea-run browns.

I was awakened the first morning by the honking of geese. Peering out of the window I saw three geese winging upstream in the daybreak fog. So at breakfast I said to Lenny, "Geese are creatures of habit. They probably will be there tomorrow morning. I would like to be there, too, with a shotgun so we can have wild goose for supper. Got a shotgun?"

"Sure," Lenny replied, and he came up with a doublebarrel classic which he handed me, plus two shells. "That's all you'll be needing," he said.

The next morning I was on the bridge at first light. Suddenly, upstream, I heard the sound of ducks quacking, taking off and heading my way. I could barely make them out in the overhead fog but I fired one shot and killed both ducks. One dropped onto the bridge while the other fell in the river.

I ran to the lodge and picked up a bait casting rig which had on an ABU Toby spoon. Running down to the nearest casting platform I waited until the duck floated past. The third cast I hooked it in the neck and retrieved it.

When Lenny came for breakfast he saw arrayed on the front porch, two mallards, the shotgun, one shell, and the baitcasting rig.

"What's the story," he queried. "One shot, three casts, two ducks, and one shell left over," I replied. And he retorted: "I should have known better than to ask!"

AT THE HEIGHT of the Vietnam war, the head Cajun visited the Pentagon in Washington. He told the first official he met: "Ah'm de haid Cajun and got an idea for winding up dat dere Vietnam war in t'irty days. I need speak to de haid jenerale."

The man replied: "Go down this hall to the door with five stars over it. That's the head general."

The head Cajun entered the door and said to the man there: "Ah'm de haid Cajun and got an idea how to wind up dat dere Vietnam war in t'irty days." "I'm listening," replied the general.

The head Cajun explained: "You give me two t'ousand dem dere Browning shootem-fast rifles, plenty ammunition, and I load up two t'ousand crazy Cajuns with guns and ammo...and Ah'm tole dem der crazy Cajuns t'ree t'ings: "One: dem dere Vietcong are easy to clean, good to eat. Two: de limit is two. And, t'ree: de season went out last Satiddy. We wipe dem out in t'irty days fo' sho'!"

• • • • • • • • • • • • • • • •

KEEPER MEMORY: Speaking of Loo-ziana, when the Outdoor Writers Association of America held its annual convention in that state, I went bass fishing with a Cajun friend.

After an enjoyable day afloat we went to his home where his wife had prepared a typical crawdad boil. They were piled up in a huge platter, looking red and ready. A pony of beer was handy to cool off the hot seasoning you could smell.

Never having eaten crawdads before, I watched my barrel-chested friend for procedure. He broke one in two, used his thumb to scoop out the mess in the crawdad's chest, sucked the goop off his thumb, smacked his lips, and made a slightly distasteful grimace.

"Do you realize what makes up that stuff?" I asked. He grinned and replied: "I do fo' sho, it's a mess. But about every tenth one tastes yummy, and that's the one you keep goin' for!"

THIS TEXAS catfish fisherman heard about the whopper blue catfish in Maine, so he journeyed there to pursue his hobby. At the moment he was leaving the dock, a typical native was just sitting down to fish for bullheads. They nodded at each other, and the Texan took off. He anchored in the middle of the lake, pulled a huge sharp hook from his kit, and baited it with a grapefruit-size hunk of bloody beef liver.

He fished fruitlessly for several hours and was just ready to give it up when he got a pickup. He set the hook and after a stiff battle he hauled in a 45-pound blue catfish. He flopped it in the boat and took off for the dock.

Just as he arrived the native had just caught his dozenth bullhead, all about banana size for good eating. He laid them on the dock just as the Texan climbed up the ladder.

The Texas flung the big blue alongside the dozen small bullheads and effused: "Well, podnuh, whaddaya think of that for a catfish, hey?" And the Mainelander replied: "Ay-yeh, just caught the one, eh?"

• • • • • • • • • • • • • • • • •

CHARLEY GILLHAM spent a major portion of his colorful life in Alaska. He covered much of the 49th state in a sled pulled by a dozen huskies. He said this experience taught him two things.

One, you make coffee or tea in the morning by melting snow, and with 12 dogs around you have to make certain the snow is white, not yellow. Also, if he should be reincarnated as a sled dog, he would make certain he would be the lead dog. That's the only one with a good view!

CHARLEY TOLD THIS STORY at an annual convention of International Game and Fish Commissioners and had them on the edges of their chairs...until the final sentence. This was typical of Gillham.

He got $25 a pelt as a government wolf trapper when that was a week's salary in the lower 48. His route covered several hundred square miles so he had built line shacks for overnight shelter.

He set up his trapping route by first flying low over it in a slow-soaring Piper cub, after a big snow. He used fist-size balls made up of rancid seal oil, corn meal, and cyanide pellets. He would fly low and fire these into the soft snow at intervals. When a hungry wolf dug down and bit into the pellet, it died instantly.

When Charley came along with his dog team, the carcasses were easy to espy against the white snow. He piled them into his sled and removed the pelts at the next line shack where he would spend the night.

His epic tale evolves around one run where he saw a chinook storm approaching. He knew the temperature drop could be severe enough to be life threatening. Knowing the nearest line cabin was too far away, his eye caught a big, aged moose grazing nearby. In a desperation move, he shot the moose just as the chinook blew in, dropping the temperature and chill factor to 40 or 50 degrees below zero. Quickly, he unharnessed the sled dogs knowing they could fend for themselves. Then he disembowled the huge moose and removed the entrails. He crawled inside the body cavity, curled his body in a fetal position to conserve heat and wait out the storm.

It blew for hours and Charley slept fitfully, awakening to peer through the belly slit at the blowing snow, then dozing off. Suddenly the wind ceased and as conciousness slowly returned he was aware of the moose's carcass being jerked. He peered out through the slit and saw two giant Arctic wolves biting off mouthfuls of meat. When they became gorged they lay down and fell asleep. Strangely, their tails were crossed as they dozed.

Charley had tried to push open the slit but found it was frozen solid and he was imprisoned inside the cavity. At that moment a survival idea lit up his hopes. Reaching out through the slit the hungry wolves had enlarged, he grabbed a wolf tail in each hand and jerked hard.

Those giant wolves leaped to their feet and took off across the snow, dragging Charley inside the frozen moose carcass. As Charley related the tale, he discovered if he let up on one wolf tail and pulled hard on the other, he could steer the moose left or right. He knew there was a rocky creek bottom close by so he steered the moose into it, letting the wolves pull the carcass over the rocks until the frictional heat softened the frozen meat. He let go the wolf tails, watched them disappear from sight, then pushed open the cavity and crawled out.

Charley concluded the tale by observing that this was the first time in the history of man that two huge Arctic wolves were terrified by a frozen moose and a frantic trapper! Wherever Charley is spending eternity, he's spinning yarns like this.

• • • • • • • • • • • • • • • • •

THIS QUAIL TALE involves an aging hunter in his 70's with an equally old bird dog, both hanging onto their bittersweet sport despite the toll of years. A younger companion was thoroughly enjoying a day afield with both.

It was almost dark and the younger hunter said: "Josh, I got my ten birds and you lack only two, so the next point is yours. Probably our last because we're just about out of light." Old Bell came through at that moment with a beautifully staunch point. Ol' Josh eased past her, kicked a grass hummock and out flushed two birds. Josh fired twice, both birds dropped dead.

"Fetch, Bell," he chortled. Bell came off point and began vacuuming the ground for a scent. She picked up a bird and brought it to Josh. "Good girl, Bell, goooood girl! Now fetch that other quaily bird, girl!" Bell fanned out, stopped, picked up the bird, and flung it to the ground.

"C'mon, Bell, fetch that bird to me, hear?!" But Bell refused by turning her head away. Josh picked up the bird, both hunters noting it wasn't a quail.

Josh sighed and put the bird in his game vest. The younger hunter said: "Josh, wasn't that a meadow lark?" And Josh replied: "Yep. Y'see, I live by the rule...if I kill it, I eat it."

His companion asked: "Ever kill a meadow lark before?" And Josh replied: "Yep, shore have."

"Well, I'm curious, what did it taste like," asked the younger man. Josh cocked his head, pondered a few moments, and mused: "Umm, maybe owl."

●●●●●●●●●●●●●●●●●

KEEPER MEMORY: I had a half day to spare on a trip through Arkansas, so I stopped by Brady Mountain Lodge well run by Reed Landis, son of the crusty, old baseball commissioner, Kennesaw Mountain Landis.

Reed was a chip off the old block, and ran a tight ship. I told him I had a few hours and never had fished Lake Ouachita, so I'd like a good guide whose brain I could pick for an article while we caught some bass and walleyes. Reed said: "Only one is available, PeeWee Wadsworth, because he's down with a migraine. Let's see how he's doing."

PeeWee said he was on the mend enough to take me, so we took off minutes later. Fishing was very slow, only yearling bass.

A beautiful shore came up with numerous deadfalls. I chunked a Chugger surface lure to the back end of a fallen tree, but before I could work it PeeWee said: "Hold it, don't move it until I tell you, hear?" I nodded, and waited at least a minute, which is a long time when you're topwater fishing. Finally he said softly: "Okay, now twitch it."

I did, and kapow, a big bass blew it out of the water and caught it on the way down! We fished for another hour with no results from normal manipulations. Then, up came another fallen tree. I laid the Chugger at the back end, PeeWee

WIFE READING husband's weight card to him: "It says:'You are handsome, a leader of men, brave, strong, and popular with the ladies, and a great fisherman as well as an intrepid hunter.'" She then added: "It's got your weight wrong, too!"

held up his hands, and I said: "I know, not until you tell me." He nodded.

Another longish wait until he whispered: "Okay, now!" I twitched the lure and a hefty bass blasted it, just as before. This quirk was repeated four times that afternoon and tallied the only bass we caught.

As we ate supper I kept waiting for PeeWee to reveal something, but he did not offer, so I didn't press him. I figured he would lay it on me when he got ready.

Six years later when Toledo Bend Lake, in Texas, got hotter than a griddle for lots of bass, I stopped at a marina and asked the manager if he had a good guide who could help me get a story. "Only one, and he's been down with a headache. Wait'll I phone him." I heard him say: "Got a feller here named Homer Circle who wants to do a story. How you feelin'? You will? Okay." He said PeeWee'd be right down.

PeeWee took me to all his good spots and we caught 26 picturesque bass that afternoon. I got good action shots, and matching article. During supper, I had to ask: "PeeWee, you remember Lake Ouachita and those bass that hit on your command. Care to tell me about it?"

PeeWee grinned one-sidedly and replied: "Uncle Homer, I knew you were gonna ask about them bass. Y'see, I was just tryin' to be funny because fishing was so slow. When it worked the first time, I was more surprised than you. And when it worked the other times, it just blew my mind. I didn't dare tell you it was a fluke and spoil our day. I've thought about it a hundred times since, and I'll tell you what. I've decided it was just meant to happen to two fishin' buddies."

I have no explanation. I just remember, and grin!

• • • • • • • • • • • • • • • • • •

A LOVABLE LITTLE CAMP COOK in far north Saskatchewan fed us well and told droll stories like this one. Two fishing buddies met and one had two black eyes.

"Whereja get 'em" asked the one. "Sunday morning, in

church," the blemished one replied. "We were in our usual seat and two newcomers sat in the pew in front of us. When the lady got up to sing a song out of the hymnal, I noticed her dress was tucked tightly inside her buns. So, trying to be helpful I reached over and pulled it out. Like that, she hit me in my right eye with her hymnal.

"Later on we got up to sing the last psalm, and I noticed her skirt was hanging straight down. Well, I knew darn well she didn't like it that way, so I reached over and with the side of my hand I tucked it back between her buns. And she hit me in my left eye with her hymnal. You know something? There are some people you can't please no matter how hard you try to help."

• • • • • • • • • • • • • • • • •

AN EBULLIENT TEXAN went to Alaska to catch some braggin' size fish. Way past his expectations he caught a 75 pound king salmon. At the bar that night be was telling about his whopper and the barkeep replied: "Well, fella, everything in Alaska is bigger than Texas. If we divided Alaska in half then Texas would be the third largest state."

"Yeah, yeah," retorted the Texan, "so I been hearing. How about a small beer?" The bartender brought him a glass of beer which held at least a quart. "I asked for a small beer," snorted the Texan. "That is a small beer in Alaska," replied the bartender. "Remember, everything is bigger in Alaska."

Later the Texan ordered a small steak. One came which filled a large platter. "I know," said the Texan, "everything is bigger in Alaska."

Later, full of beer, he asked where the men's room was. "Second door down the hall," he was told. Woozy, he went in the third door, staggered into a big, dark room and fell into a swimming pool. He could be plainly heard, shouting at the top of his voice: "DOOON'T FLUSH IT!"

JUGFISHING FOR CATFISH for a living is a tough way to cut it, but that's the way Eefie Crockett made his living. He'd go below the dam in his johnboat, bait up a hook suspended from the ear on a plastic jug, and toss it overboard. He may have out as many as twenty jugs planted in pockets along the shoreline. He'd run his holes, marking them with a rag tied on a bush.

On good days he'd come home whistlin' happy and was nice to be around. But on skunked days he was miserable company. Elvie, his wife, solved it with a wifely wile. She asked Eefie to put a little moonshine in each jug, and swear on his mother's bible he would take a nip only when there was no catfish on the jug.

It was a perfect solution. On days when Eefie caught a lot of catfish, he came home elated with success. And on days when he caught nothing, he'd come home empty handed but happy as a drunk skunk! And that was an end result Elvie could live with.

All of which goes to prove an old saw: "For every woman who makes a fool out of a man, there are a thousand women who make a man out of a fool!"

• • • • • • • • • • • • • • • • •

MUSKIE FISHERMEN are a breed apart from all other anglers. I emphasized this when I spoke at a national muskie symposium in Lacrosse, Wisconsin. I reminded them of the unusual psyche which possesses their clan.

For instance... After a hard day's pursuit of the world's toughest game fish to catch, devotees would meet at the local pub to check out each fisherman's day. You'd see a crowd around ol' Olie because someone said he had two "follows." Mind you, he didn't catch one muskie, just had two follow in his lures. They would ask Olie where he was fishing, what lures he used, how he was working them, what time of day did the action occur, etc.

Suddenly, the crowd would leave Olie and huddle around Sven. Sven, by golly, had four follows, yah-sure he did. Didn't catch a cottonpickin' fish, just had four follows, and he was the man of the hour!

I reminded them of the time Christ fed the multitude on two fish. And bet them not a person in the audience would believe these two fish were muskies. Even Christ would be too wise to expect to catch two muskies on such short notice.

● ● ● ● ● ● ● ● ● ● ● ● ● ● ● ● ●

A FISHERMAN had been chunking big plugs for muskies all morning without so much as a follow. Disgusted, he decided to halt for lunch and pulled over under the shade of a mammoth sycamore tree.

As he munched a sandwich, he happened to glance at the root of the big tree, and was puzzled to see a hickory nut right at the water's edge. As he pondered what was a hickory nut doing beneath a sycamore tree, he saw a squirrel scramble down the tree and crawl up to the nut. At that moment a huge muskie shot from the water, seized the squirrel in its toothy jaws, and disappeared from sight. He hardly believed what he had just seen and wished he could have filmed it. Again, he wondered how that nut got there. At that moment he saw a big swirl close by the same root. Out of the swirl emerged the big, toothy head of the muskie and it gently put the hickory nut back on the root. You and I laugh. Muskie fishermen say: "What is so funny about that logical experience?"

● ● ● ● ● ● ● ● ● ● ● ● ● ● ● ● ●

THE ONLY WEEKEND this rabid angler didn't go fishing was the one when he got married and went on his honeymoon. They were headed for his remote fishing cabin in the hill country when it started to rain in torrents. There was a stretch of road which was dirt, and it became so slippery their tires had no traction. So the groom said: "Honey, we've got to use

29

our clothes to put down to make our tires hold, or we'll be stranded here all night. Let's start with your bridal gown." Reluctantly she took off the gown. He put it under the rear wheels and they gained a few feet. Next, he used her slip, bra, and panties to gain a couple more yards. Then came his $500 country-western outfit, his underwear, plus his ten-gallon hat, to gain several more feet. They were just a few feet from the pavement and the only item left was his lizard cowboy boots. "Honey," he said, "tell you what...these boots cost a thousand bucks, and I just can't part with them. But, I've got an idea. See that light up there? Someone's home in that little cabin. Take these boots with you and see if you can make a deal for them to tow us out of this mess."

In her birthday suit she made her way through rain to the cabin door. She knocked and before an oldtimer opened the door, she covered her nudity by placing the uppers of the cowboy boots between her legs, with just the soles and heels showing. Grasping the boot bottoms between her hands, she looked up at the oldtimer, smiling.

He cocked his head and said: "Something wrong, m'am?" And she came back: "Yes, you see, we're on our honeymoon and my husband got stuck!" The oldtimer looked her over with a quizzical eye and queried: "Well, ma'm, have you tried holding your nose and blowing?"

• • • • • • • • • • • • • • • • •

AT A REMOTE FISHING lodge in far-north Canada a guest asked the owner: "Well, what's the weather look like for tomorrow?" And the manager replied: "I learned long ago never to predict weather in this remote latitude, but I have a suggestion. Take the path to the right at the bottom of the hill and ask the old Indian chief in the tepee, he's uncanny in the accuracy of his weather predictions."

So, the guest visited the venerable old chief and said: "I understand you are the weatherman in these parts. What's the weather going to be like tomorrow?" And the old chief said: "Tomorrow it rain, rain all day. You take rain coat fishing." Sure enough, it rained from dawn to dark as predicted. And that evening the guest again visited the old chief who opined: "Tomorrow big wind blow too hard to fish. Better stay in lodge." It was just that kind of day. That evening he again asked the old chief about tomorrow's weather. The old chief replied: "Dunno." And the guest probed: "What do you mean, you dunno?" The chief came back: "Dunno, radio busted!"

•••••••••••••••••

WHILE ON INDIANS, the old chief's young son came to him and asked: "Oh my venerable father, I must ask you a question. Where do we Indians get our funny names?"

"It is good that you should be inquiring about such matters, my son. These names come from an ancient custom in our tribe. We choose them from whatever notable event is taking place at the moment of birth. Take your sister, Running Deer. A deer ran past the tepee as she was birthed. And your brother Barking Dog...it is obvious where his name came from. And my name, Rising Sun, that was when I was born. But, tell me, Moose Breaking Wind, is there some question about your name?"

•••••••••••••••••

THREE OLD TRAPPERS were sitting in their line cabin shooting the breeze before retiring. One said: "A curious question occurs to me. What is the most horrible sound ever in the world?" One oldtimer said: "I've heard it. It was the terrible gurgling noise which came from the throat of a man I watched get hung for stealing horses."

The second trapper said: "Well, I think I heard a more horrible sound than that one time. "I saw a man get grabbed by a huge grizzly b'ar and that b'ar not only squeezed him to a slow death, but it also scalped him with its monstrous teeth. His dying cry just curled my hair. Never forget it. Got to be the most horrible sound."

"Nope," retorted the third old trapper. "I will tell you the second most horrible sound I ever heard. This here then trapping buddy of mine had to go outside for a BM, and he happened to squat down on top of a big bear trap I had chained down that morning because one was prowling around our cabin. When those trap jaws slammed shut on his you-know-what, it was the second most horrible sound I ever expect to hear.

"Well, if that was the second most horrible sound, I'd like to know just what was the most horrible sound you've heard?" And the old trapper replied: "When he hit the end of that chain!"

• • • • • • • • • • • • • • • • • •

INDIAN TRIBAL WISDOM has always impressed me with its simple truths. On one overnight stay in LaRonge, Saskatchewan, while having an ale at the quaint lodge restaurant, I overheard this quote attributed to a local chief:

"If you would soar with the eagles on the morrow...don't hoot too long with the owls tonight!" And on our way to the gravel-strip airport the next morning I took a picture of an inscription over the entrance to the Cree tribe burial grounds. It hangs on my office wall, and the letters carved into a weathered plank read: "If we could not as brothers live, let us here as brothers lie." Not a bad thought for men of all nations!

Our two guides for two couples on that trip were named Sandy and Alex. Our two wives felt at ease with the two Crees because they were both quiet and attentive to our needs. Typical of the intelligence of these Indians was an incident which occured during our shore lunch. We were eating walleye fillets and fried potatoes. I just happened to look down at the mound I was standing on, totally made up of seeds.

I was curious about where so many seeds could have derived from in this remote site. So, I asked Sandy: "Where did all these seeds come from?" Sandy looked at Alex for at least

THE OLD HUNTER was out walking his just-bought German Shepherd when he met a friend. "Hey," he beamed, "look what I just got for my wife." And his friend replied: "Wish I could make a trade like that!"

a minute, and because he was not too fluent in English, we knew he was thinking. Finally, he smiled and replied: "Seeds been through bear." It doesn't take education to be a gentleman around ladies. It does take desire and a gentility which compliment the moment.

•••••••••••••••••

KEEPER MEMORIES: Ed Zern, Field and Stream's long-running outdoor humorist and gentle man whose comradeship I cherish, is blessed with a quiet, unique wit which has lightened the moments of millions of readers. Let me share these Zern memories with you.

We met on a fishing safari on Brazil's Amazon River and had spent a sweltering morning fishing for native species. We came in for lunch and were basking in the shade provided by a palm-thatched roof on a two-story houseboat. Cooling drinks were being enjoyed by parched members of this Braniff Airlines exploratory cruise.

Also a member of this group was Jim Crowe, veteran outdoor editor of the Detroit News. Zern had unbuttoned his shirt and was holding a cold Scotch mist against his chest, with a big smile on his face and eyes closed in peace. Mark Sosin popped through the door and asked, in his stentorian voice: "Has anyone seen Crowe?" Zern opened one eye and offered: "Crowe? Crowe? Well, he's probably out harassing an owl." The one open eye closed to resume his reverie.

At that moment, the African Queen, as we had dubbed her, shifted in her mooring. A shaft of sunlight lit up Zern's navel like a spotlight in that shaded room. My camera was handy so I quietly zoomed in on one of the ugliest navels I could remember, shooting several closeups.

Upon returning home I had the sharpest one enlarged to an 8x10 color print. That year, at the annual convention of the Outdoor Writers Association of America I hung the picture by a table with a sign: "What does this look like to you? A prize will be awarded to the best description."

Fellow journalists came through with some vivid descriptions. I remember these... "The east end of a cat walking west;" "A fur ball upchucked by a great horned owl;" "My unshaven Uncle Clem with his teeth out trying to keep from laughing at one of my bon mots." I awarded the prize to one which referred to the locale of a memorable historical site, Campo Bello, where Roosevelt, Stalin, and Churchill met for the post WWII peace conference. The winning title was: "Sunrise at Campo Belly-O."

Believing Zern would be interested in what his fellow scribes thought his navel looked like, I sent the entire batch to him, together with the picture. Shortly thereafter I received this terse note from him: "Thanks for your thoughtfulness... but I really don't deem it a very good likeness."

• • • • • • • • • • • • • • • • •

ON ONE OF OUR fishing trips Zern shared this keeper memory with me. He was fishing in the far north, his only companion an Athabaska Indian guide. They had been together for a week and although the Indian spoke very little English, by now they were fishing buddies, getting by on spare words, nods, smiles, and hand signals.

Suddenly, here it was, their last evening together, tomorrow was departure day. Now Zern knew, as all there must learn, you never give an Indian alcohol in any form. They appear to believe an opened bottle is meant to be emptied. But on this special occasion, Zern had poured two small paper cups with wine he had brought along for the occasion. Handing one to his new buddy, Zern smiled over his extended cup and said: "Salute!" The Indian smiled across his extended cup and said: "Sal-loot!"

Then, Zern noticed the Indian frowning and thinking, as if some words were struggling to get out. Zern kept smiling to encourage him, then, tilting his head, he hesitantly asked: "Where...you...from?" Zern grinned, extended his cup, took a sip, and replied in the same meter: "New...York...City."

The Indian shook his head, blinking his eyes in thought as he observed Zern across the campfire's flickering illuminance...some words obviously forming in his mind. Zern smiled, and nodded his head in encouragement.

Raising his eyebrows in question, the Indian said slowly: "New...York...City?..hmnnn. What... big... town...that...near?"

• • • • • • • • • • • • • • • • • •

FINALLY, TYPICALLY ZERN, here is an experience he shared during a reminiscing session together. He was asked to speak before an large audience, and shared the program with three other speakers. Zern was asked to cap the evening with his humor. But the EmCee did a very poor job of holding the preceeding speakers to their allotted 20 minutes. Each was drier than a popcorn hiccup and by the time Zern was introduced, he expertly read his audience as bored, disinterested, and many were yawning, struggling to stay awake.

When Zern took the mike, he gave his broadest bearded smile, paused overly long as he casually scanned each segment, and said: "Ladies and gentlemen, the evening has been very lengthy and you have been very patient. I have decided to change my topic. I'm going to speak on...SEX!"

Many heads perked up immediately, amid whispers and smiles. He paused, nestled close to the mike and said with fervor: "It's WONderful!" He got a standing ovation. Long live that oner, Zern!

• • • • • • • • • • • • • • • • • •

THREE GRIZZLY STORIES The fisherman was totally absorbed trying to "match the hatch" for trout in a remote Alaskan stream. Suddenly a roar shocked him into alertness, and he looked downstream to see a huge grizzly rushing at him, teeth gnashing.

He dropped his fly rod and streaked to the nearest sizable tree. He scaled it in nothing flat. The grizzly tried to climb,

CANNIBAL TO CHIEF: "I think your wife makes the very best soup I have ever tasted!" The chief takes a spoonful and replies: "Yep, I agree. I sure am gonna miss that gal!"

couldn't make it, but kept roaring and gnashing, biting the bark off the tree, shaking it with mighty forelegs, trying to dislodge the man. When he saw he was safe, he got mad and began pelting the big bear with pine cones. The grizzly roared back, defiantly, then slowly ambled away, bellowing and glaring back at him. He waited a spell, and decided it was time to descend and head for camp.

Just then he heard two roars and over the rise came the huge grizzly with an equally big companion. They both rushed up to the tree, shook it hard trying to dislodge him, chewed big chunks out of the base, snarling and roaring up at him. He never imagined such ferocity and determination to get at him from wild bears.

Again, he got mad back and with as much strength as he could muster with his free arm he pounded them both with the biggest pine cones he could reach. Each time he hit one it roared up at him, showing all its dentures, and pawing the air.

At long last they stopped trying to demolish the tree base and sashayed off, looking back and bawling defiantly. After a spell, feeling he had scored a moral victory, he began shinnying down the pine tree. He halted when he heard two roars from beyond the hill, climbed back to his safe perch, and smiled, confident he could outwait them until the lodge would miss him and send an armed guide. Suddenly, the two giant grizzlies again loomed into view. Only this time, they brought along two beavers!

• • • • • • • • • • • • • • • • •

TWO WILDLIFE PHOTOGRAPHERS were on a picture shooting trek in northern Canada. The older one heard a loud roar, looked down the trail and saw a monster grizzly tearing toward them. The younger, less experienced shuttersnapper stared aghast and asked: "What in the world are we gonna do?" And the older photog replied: "Dunno, but let's each get camera ready. One of us is gonna get one helluvan action shot!"

TWO OTHER PHOTOGS, same area and scene, whopper grizzly dashing at them. The younger photog whipped off his backpack, got out his gym shoes and began switching them with his heavy boots. The older photog quizzed: "You don't think you can outrun that big, mean grizzly, do you?" "Nope," retorted the younger one, "just keep ahead of you!"

● ● ● ● ● ● ● ● ● ● ● ● ● ● ● ● ●

WHAT'S BREEZY and smells like worms? When a spring robin flatulates and you're downwind!

● ● ● ● ● ● ● ● ● ● ● ● ● ● ● ● ●

A YOUNG CITY FELLER got lost in the hills, saw a light, knocked on the door, it opened and the old man said: "Welcome, you're lost, or you wouldn't be knockin' on our door, and ma's just settin' the table, so why not join us for a bite of supper so we can get acquainted?" The young man couldn't refuse such a cordial and logical invitation, so he joined them.

It was a delightful country-cooked meal he thoroughly enjoyed. While they chatted, ma did up the dishes then joined them to sit, knit, and rock. Suddenly the old man said: "You'll have to pardon me, son, but boiled cabbage really makes me gassy." And with that he cut loose with a real thunderboomer. Instantly, two big coon dogs leaped through an open window and the curtains flowed outward as they disappeared.

Puzzled, the young man asked: "Sir, when you let that one go, almost as if by signal, both dogs took off through that window. Why?" And the old man replied: "Guess that would puzzle a stranger, son, but you see ma's hard of hearin' and when she smells a stench she gets up and kicks hell out of the dogs!"

AT THE CAPE CANAVERAL space station, two guards were chatting during the night shift. One was new on the job and about midnight he asked: "Time sure drags by. Ain't nuthin' a guy can do to help time pass faster?" And the other said: "Yes, but don't blab it around. Lemme show you." So they went to the big lab and the oldtimer said: "This jug contains space fuel. It's potent stuff and only takes a small sip, so go easy."

Both had a few sips, and the newcomer slipped back later for a few more. Sure enough, the night did pass faster...and so did the new guard who phoned the next morning, saying: "I say, good buddy, remember that space fuel we drank last night? Just how do you feel?" And the older guard replied: "Well, to tell you the truth, I drank a little too much, and I feel gassy, r-e-a-l gassy." "Me, too, and that's why I phoned to warn you. If you pass gas, don't light up a cigarette." "No?" asked the other, "Why not?" And the answer came back: "Well, I did...and I'm phonin' you from Seattle!"

• • • • • • • • • • • • • • • • •

WE WERE ENJOYING some delightful giant brook trout fishing at a God's Lake in Manitoba. All was well, except on a 1 to 10 scale our Indian guide was barely a four. But, he was pleasant. Keep in mind he had been guiding some ten years, so he did know where big fish hung out. And he knew two speeds on the 50 horse Merc, dead still and wide open.

Many Indians take their names from famous people; his was Churchill. He rarely used a paddle and was usually dozing when the situation called for one. We kibitzed his shore lunch cookery or he'd put onions in everything including the coffee, and burn anything in the skillet. Churchill is easily forgettable except for one moment during our final fishing day, on our way out. He was roaring along wide open, as usual, Childbride and I facing him on the front seat, backs to the chilly wind. Suddenly we were hurled rearward as the motor skeg made a horrible noise as it dragged for some 50 feet over solid rock,

then dropped off the far edge. Churchill gave us a deadpan look, nodded, and said: "Rock still there!" It made for a lighthearted day!

● ● ● ● ● ● ● ● ● ● ● ● ● ● ● ● ● ●

THIS RABID quail hunter heard about a faultless pointer that never failed to find birds. So he journeyed to South Dakota to check it out, and possibly buy it at any price. He hired the owner and dog for a day and the only stipulation was that the owner got to hunt also, including the first point.

They weren't in the field two minutes when the faultless pointer came down solid. The owner walked past him, a covey hit the sky and the owner fired three times with three quail dropping dead. The faultless pointer retrieved each one, and as he handed each to the owner he licked his boot.

The next point belonged to the hunter, so he strolled past the faultless pointer, flushed the cove, fired three times and two birds dropped. The faultless pointer retrieved each one, flung it at the hunter's feet, and peed in his boot. The same scenario took place again, the owner hitting three for three, birds retrieved, boot licked. Hunter: one out of three shots, bird retrieved, flung at his feet, both boots peed in.

And the hunter blew his cool. He strode to face the owner and carped: "Why that is the most exasperating, insulting bird dog I've ever seen. I'd never buy such a canine smartass. Why in the world do you put up with him?" And the owner replied: "Why do you think I'm such a deadly shot? I just can't stand soggy boots!"

• • • • • • • • • • • • • • • • •

IN THE SAME VEIN, a hunter stopped in a store to pick up some beef jerky. As he emerged he noticed a little, old lady being pulled along by her seeing-eye dog. He stood still, curious to see how the dog would handle the traffic light. The canny dog looked up at the green light, stopped dead still, then lifted his leg and tinkled in the little old lady's shoe. She calmly reached into her shoulder bag and came out with a dog biscuit. Reaching down she handed it to the dog who promptly chomped away. He rushed out and said: "M'am, don't reward that miserable dog, he'll just do it again!" And the little old lady replied: "Why you silly fool, I'm not rewarding him...I'm just trying to locate his head so I can kick his butt off!"

• • • • • • • • • • • • • • • • •

KEEPER MEMORY "Big George" Cook, all 250 pounds of him, was an Arkansas fishing and hunting buddy. On our first duck hunt he had built a tree blind and we were sitting there, chatting, trying to ignore the bluebird day which presaged no ducks airborne. To kill time, I said to Big George: "Show me how you use those two duck calls hanging around your neck." He replied: "This big one is my highball call which

I use when to get their attention from far off. And this little feller is my chuckle, or feeding call when they get close enough to coax in." I suggested: "Get on that highball and see if you can coax one out of that big marsh." He did, so loud it hurt my eardrums. But in the north I spotted a lone duck, headed our way. "Give the feeding call," I urged. He did, and that lone duck headed over our blind. I killed it clean, retrieved it, and noticed a band on its leg. "What's it say," he asked. I read the wording: Bio Sta. Joplin, MO, to him. Big George allowed: "Tell you what, I've called ducks from a fur piece over the years, but this'n is my best yet!"

● ● ● ● ● ● ● ● ● ● ● ● ● ● ● ● ● ● ●

ODE TO A REDBUG
A chigger, I figger
Ain't much bigger
Than a dot on the head of a pin;
But its bite is a fright,
And you scratch all night,
Aye, that's where the rub comes in!

● ● ● ● ● ● ● ● ● ● ● ● ● ● ● ● ●

DOGGEREL FOR ENDEARED DOGS Some folks think dogs ain't got much sense, that they don't know what's what, but from the aquaintance I've had with dogs, I know dogs know lots. Now you kinda watch your ol' dog and from him you'll learn a lesson, treat him your best and you will find his love to be a blessin'. He'll stick to you through thick and thin and when you're down and out and filled with sorrow, he'll wag his tail as if to say, "Cheer up, better luck tomorrow."

Now friends, when I die should I reach the pearly gates and find there a sign...No Dogs Allowed...by gosh I'll hesitate. For should my old dog be standing there and look me in the face...I'm afraid I'll have to take a chance and try the other place!

43

THE VETERAN DUCK HUNTER was in his blind before daybreak, everything in its place, waiting for daybreak to bring mallards to his neatly "J-hook" decoy arrangement.

At first light he could barely hear the hunter in the next blind humming...as he looked he could see light glint from an upended bottle. He couldn't believe anyone would violate the fundamental rule of no booze while hunting. Next he heard the man singing in falsetto, then came some loud snoring.

The sun rose very bright and he knew ducks would be scarce. After a couple blank hours, he saw one duck winging his way at least 60 yards high. He took a desperation shot but missed. As the lofty duck passed over the drinking hunter's blind, he saw him jump up, heard him snort, fire one shot, and down the duck came, stone dead. He couldn't help applaud the marksmanship, so he hollered: "Great shot, I've never seen a better one!" "Oh, I dunno" (hiccup) replied the other hunter, "I us-us-burp-usually get two 'er three outuva flo-flo-flock like that!"

• • • • • • • • • • • • • • • • • •

THE NOTED EVANGELIST had reached the crescendo in his sermon, hair mussed, arms waving, striding across the platform, saying: "I know God looks after me day and night. Why when I get up in the middle of the night to go to the bathroom, God turns on the light for me...and when I'm through God turns off the light for me. That's how well God looks after me. And He'll look after you, too, if you believe fervently enough!"

A reporter sitting beside the evangelist's wife said: "M'am, I can't help but ask the question: Does God look after you, too, like he does your husband? Does He turn on the bathroom light for you, then turn it off when you're through?" She smiled and replied: "No, I must be honest. God doesn't do those things for me. But, then, I don't get up in the middle of the night and stumble/fumble around and tinkle in the refrigerator, either!"

MY FAVORITE ALL-TIME fishing cartoon showed two fishermen silhouetted by a shoreside fire, sipping coffee. The cutlines read: "What is there about the lapping of clear water on squeaky-clean rocks, the soughing of wind and wild cry of a loon that makes campfire coffee taste so lousy!"

• • • • • • • • • • • • • • • • • •

FATHER MAHONEY had been the priest at this small parish for 25 years, and was about to retire so he could find more time to pursue his favorite hobby, fishing. Yet, he resisted yielding any authority to young Father O'Rielly before the final day. On the Sunday of his final sermon he got in a couple barbs by saying: "Remember Father O'Rielly is quite untempered with only a year's tutoring under me. But, be patient, in due time he will become passable."

All watching Father O'Rielly saw the crimson in his face suddenly match the red in his hair, and wondered if his Irish temper might not trigger a rebuttal. Time came for his acceptance sermon and he wound up with these words. "I'd like to address my remarks to the young people in our congregation. You know, sin has a terrible price. Why, as much as you love your father, if he sins he can go to hell. And if your dear mother should sin, she can go to hell. Then pointing his finger at his mentor he said in a loud, clear voice: "Even Father Mahoney can go to hell!"

• • • • • • • • • • • • • • • • • •

KEEPER MEMORY: I was flying the bush so much in single engine aircraft, I learned to fly a plane, just in case I ever had to land one in an emergency. This event took place at the airport in Rogers, Arkansas, told to me by my instructor George Muschany.

The janitor was a very pleasant man in his 50's, the only name I heard him called was Herman. One day one of the veteran pilots said: "Herman, how about going with me this afternoon, I have to fly to Joplin and back. I think you'll enjoy it!

"Oh, no sir, thank you, but I'd rather not," Herman replied.

"Now Herman, I know you're a fatalist because I overheard you say you believed a man would live until it came his time to go, and that would be it. So you shouldn't be afraid to fly if you still believe that. Do you?"

"Yessir, I sure do. With all my heart!" he replied.

"Well, then, what are you afraid of?" asked the pilot. And Herman came back very slowly: "Well, suppose just you and me are up there flying along at 10,000 feet...and it comes your time to go!"

● ● ● ● ● ● ● ● ● ● ● ● ● ● ● ● ● ● ●

THREE MEN OF THE CLOTH were fishing one day and lunch time rolled around. The Rabbi said: "I'm hungry, where's the food?" And Father Callahan replied: "I'll be glad to get it from the car." So saying he stepped overboard, scampered over the water, jumped ashore, got the lunch basket, scampered back to the boat and climbed aboard.

Looking in the basket Father Callahan said: "Bejabbers, I forgot the cold drinks." And the Methodist Minister said: "Let me get them, Father." So he scampered across the water to get the drinks, then scampered back across to climb aboard. By now, the Rabbi was wide-eyed and thinking: "I wonder if my faith will be strong enough to sustain me over that water?" Compelled to put it to the test the Rabbi said: "Let me go ashore, gentlemen, I forgot my sunglasses and need them badly." He leaped from the boat and promptly sank out of sight. Three times they helped him aboard, and three times he leaped in to sink again. Father Callahan said: "Better tell that zealot where those rocks are before he drowns himself!"

ONE ELDER OUTDOORSMAN said "oldtimer's disease" really bugged him. You know, looked for his glasses and found them on top of his head...Went out to his workshop to get a tool and when he got there he forgot which tool and what for...Looked an old friend square in the face and couldn't recall his name. But, no more does it bug him, he told me, now that he has this new philosophy: "If there's something you can't remember...what the hell... forget it!" Now he enjoys two events much more than before. One, he can help plan his own surprise birthday party. And two, he can hide his own Easter eggs!

• • • • • • • • • • • • • • • • •

SPEAKING OF REMEMBERING NAMES, I was talking with Lew Klewer, venerated outdoor editor of the Toledo Blade, then in his 80's, at the annual meet of the American Outdoor Writers Association of America. We saw most of our friends once yearly. A young man walked up, hand over name tag, and said: "Lew, what's my name?" I thought, what a dirty trick to play on ol' Lew. Lew cocked his head and responded: "Well, I remember your name... but I forget your face!"

• • • • • • • • • • • • • • • • •

WHEN I HEAR FELLOW outdoorsmen complain about "growing old"...I remind them of these certain signs to be alert for, signifying you truly are "over the hill."

*When your back goes out more than you do.

*When you reach over in the night to fondle your spouse and your hand falls asleep.

*When a pretty lass strolls by and your pacemaker makes the garage door run up and down.

*When you sit down in a rocking chair and you can't get it goin'!

*Your main exercise is being a pallbearer for friends who exercised too much.

*You sink your teeth into a steak and they stay there.

*You remember today that yesterday was your wife's birthday or your wedding anniversary.

*You're 17 around the neck, 42 around the waist, and 120 around the golf course.

*You know all the answers but nobody ever asks you any questions.

*You feel at last you've earned the right to procrastinate, but somehow never get around to it.

• • • • • • • • • • • • • • • • • •

AN OLD TEXAS COUPLE lived on a remote 40 acres with their only son. An oil drilling crew came through and offered to prospect a hole free. If they hit, a percentage of the take would be paid. They shook hands.

They drilled a 10,000-foot dry hole, no oil. So the old man said: "Tell you what, to save a total loss just leave the hole open. Don't fill it in, and I thank you." After they left the old man called his son and said: "Now let's move that outhouse for the last time over that 10,000-foot hole! No more diggin', that's time better spent out fishin'."

The next morning the old man was sitting and sipping his first coffee. The son came dashing in and said, excitedly: "Pa, pa, you better go take a look at ma. I came by the outhouse and she was sittin' there with her eyes buggin' out, and her face turnin' blue. What in the world do you suppose is wrong with her?" The old man smiled, took a sip of coffee, and replied: "Don't worry son, tain't nothin' serious. She's just gonna have to get over her old habit of holding her breath until she hears it hit bottom!"

MOSES CAME DOWN from the mountains, holding the stone tablets in his weary arms. Facing his rapt, waiting group, he said: "Got some good, some bad news. Good news: we pared all those commandments down to ten. Bad news: adultery stays in!"

FOUR MOOSE HUNTERS were on their annual trip to Alaska. This year they took a newcomer along. And they told him: "Now we draw straws to see who starts out being cook. He cooks until someone complains about the food, then the complainer stays in camp and does all the cookin'.

The newcomer somehow got the short straw. He cooked fairly well the first day just to be fair. The second day he got edgy to go moose hunting so he burned the food. A few sour faces but no complaints. The third day he really fouled up the chow by over salting everything. His three compadres gave him dirty looks, but no one complained. The fourth day he fed them raw meat, and cremated the toast. Lots of gulping down, but no complaints. With time running out and desperate to go moose hunting, for supper that night he made hamburgers mixed with moose dung he stepped in that morning. They all sat down to eat supper. One took a big bite, made a horrible face, and shouted: "This dang hamburger tastes like moose dung!" He saw all eyes bore through him so he smacked his lips, gulped, then added emphatically: "..."but GOOD!"

• • • • • • • • • • • • • • • • • •

HIS NEW NEIGHBOR turned out to be a fisherman so they made a date to go before they really ever got acquainted. Trying to be good buddy he brought along the lunch, furnished the boat, and took him to his good hole.

As they began to fish, the good guy saw his new neighbor pull out a beer can with monofilament wrapped around it, bait up a hook with chewing gum and fling it into the water. He asked: "Ever try spinfishing with a pushbutton reel?"

The neighbor replied: "Yep, tried it one time, never liked it." He went on: "Ever try baitcasting?"

The reply came back: "One time, never liked it." He pursued: "Spinning, or fly fishing?"

And the reply came back: "Tried 'em all one time, never liked 'em!"

After a quiet spell, the new neighbor finally added: "Just thought of something. My young son uses all those outfits well. You might take him out some time." And the good guy queried in a soft voice: "Your only child, I presume?"

•••••••••••••••••

THE HUNTER was hurrying home in his old pickup, trying to get there in time to clean his game before supper. Bad luck struck when he had a flat just outside the state insane asylum. He jacked up the pickup, pried off the hub cap and as he unscrewed each lug nut he carefully placed it in the inverted hub cap.

He noticed a man leaning on the asylum fence, nodding in approval as he proceeded. Just as he pushed on the spare tire he happened to kick the hub cap, and all the lug nuts fell into an open sewer grate. He said outloud: "Now what the heck am I gonna do?" The man leaning on the fence stated, matter of factly: "Well, I'd take one nut off each of the other three wheels. I'd use these to secure the spare and get me to an auto parts shop where I could buy six new nuts." The hunter grinned and said: "Hey, thanks for the suggestion. But if you can think like that what are you doing in a place like this?" And the man came back: "Well, I may be crazy, fella, but I'm not stupid!"

•••••••••••••••••

THE BEDLESS PICKUP was speeding over a back road late at night. In it were two "bubba boys" with a big hog they had stolen sitting on the floor. "Quick," said Zekie, let's prop this ol' hog between us with our elbows, and put your ball cap on his head. Those dumb deputies after us can't see too well in the dark."

They stopped the pickup and waited for the one deputy to approach them. He said to the driver: "What's your name?"

"Zekie Slapstick," was the reply. The deputy went around to the passenger side and asked the same question. The other hillbilly responded: "Eph Slapstick." Squinting at the middle passenger, the deputy pulled out his flashlight, shined it on the face of the big hog wearing the baseball cap, and asked: "And what's your name, fella?" Both hillbillies poked the propped hog in the ribs with their elbows, and the hog went, "OINK!" The deputy said: "Well, you boys watch your speed, hear?" Then he returned to the prowl car with a puzzled look, shook his head and said: "I wish you could have seen that Oink Slapstick. He's the ugliest hillbilly I ever hope to see!"

• • • • • • • • • • • • • • • • • •

THE YOUNG MAN joined the army and was sent overseas for a four-year hitch. He got homesick, phoned his father, and said: "You know, pa, I just now realize how good I had it. There are so many things I miss. Like going fishin' and huntin' together...Ma's home cookin'...Followin' ol' Blue at night chasin' those big he-coons up trees...goin' down to the ol' swimmin' hole to cool off on hot summer days. Yep, and you won't believe what else I miss a lot? It's that little ol' pot I kept under the bed." His dad came back: "Yes, son, you missed it a lot when you were home, too!"

• • • • • • • • • • • • • • • • • •

A BUNCH OF KIDS were fishing with cane poles off a dock, when one of the the little boys fell in. After a lot of hollering, they managed to pull him out. He stood there embarassed, dripping, with everybody staring at him. At that moment one of the camp directors walked up, put his arm around the lad and asked: "Son, tell me, how did you come to fall in?"

And the soggy little boy replied: "Honest, I didn't come to fall in...I came to fish!"

KEEPER MEMORIES Duffy Daugherty, who loved the outdoors almost as much as the sport of football where he made his fame, was guest speaker at a Notre Dame victory banquet. He was noted for his off-beat stories, and this one made a touchdown.

Each year, this big college football team played a charity game against a make-up squad of husky coal miners in West Virginia. This particular year it was cold, the ground was frozen hard, and the miners were down to one big sub they hoped wouldn't be needed, he was so slow-witted. Finally, another injury, and the coach called him up. "Charjewzskewitz," he said, "go in there and knock down anyone who comes through the line." "Right on, coach," he grinned and ran in.

The first play he was hit hard low, his head hit the frozen ground and he had to be taken to the hospital. He awakened, started to talk, and found his jaw was wired shut. "Hey, how'm I gonna eat?" he mumbled. The doctor said: "We'll have to feed you rectally with a funnel until your jaw heals."

"Well, what can I have to eat?" he muttered. And the nurse said: "Oh, meat broths, thin soups, tea, or hot chocolate." He thought on it, grinned through his wired teeth and said: "Hey, bring me some hot chocolate. That sounds good!" The nurse left and came back with a big pitcher of hot chocolate. She turned him on his side to administer the funnel and tube, then slowly began pouring the hot chocolate. "OOOOOOOHHHH!!!" exclaimed the footballer. The nurse asked: "What's the matter, too hot?" To which he replied: "No...too sweet!"

● ● ● ● ● ● ● ● ● ● ● ● ● ● ● ● ● ●

THE PESSIMIST had been sitting on the dock fishing since daybreak, without so much as a nibble. A fisherman boated past and said: "How you doin'?"

"Terrible," replied the docker. "Well, cheer up, friend. You're a free man, in a free nation, able to fish whenever you like, and speak your mind whenever you feel like it. Look

53

at it this way...things could be a whole lot worse." Then he smiled, waved, and rowed away. And he was right. Shortly after he left, things got worse. The docker fell in!

• • • • • • • • • • • • • • • • •

SCENARIO: Grandma and granddaughter seated on a train, headed for a day on the beach. Seated opposite them was a tough-looking sergeant and a young private, headed for boot camp.

The young private was making eyes at the pretty lass. The car blacked out when the train went through a tunnel. The only sounds heard were a kissing slurp, then a loud slap. When the train emerged into the light, the sergeant had a red, swelling eye. The grandma thought: "Bet that macho lookin' sergeant tried to kiss my granddaughter, and she socked him in the eye. Now she shouldn't have." The lass thought: "That tough-looking sergeant tried to kiss me, got grandma instead, and she popped him in the eye!" And the sergeant thought: "That lucky, young private takes advantage of the dark and kisses the young chick. She takes a swing at him, misses, and I get popped in the eye. Wait'll I get him back in boot camp." And the grinning, young private was thinking: "I hope that cocky sergeant never finds out I finally got even for all the guff he's been laying on me in camp...when I kissed the back of my hand and smacked him in the eye!"

• • • • • • • • • • • • • • • • •

TWO OLDTIMERS were in camp on an annual fishing trip and drew names as bunkbuddies. One had just got a new set of false teeth and did nothing but carp about how they hurt. It got to be a continuous diatribe.

His partner was fed up with it and saw a chance to get even when they were fishing the next day. The complainer was sitting in the seat ahead of him, facing forward. He laid his false teeth on the seat beside him, saying: "I can't stand them dadgummed choppers so I might as well fish in peace." His partner grinned, and saw his chance to get even with the carper. He swapped his own false teeth with those on the seat, putting the teeth of the carper in his own jacket pocket. Noontime came and they had brought along a couple sandwiches for lunch. The partner handed one to the carper, saw him reach down, pick up the false teeth, slip them into his mouth, and take a big bite of sandwich. He chomped down, yowled: "OWWW! That does it, I've had it, OUT damned teeth!" then threw them overboard. His partner sat with mixed emotions.

• • • • • • • • • • • • • • • • •

THIS FANATICAL FISHERMAN had promised to be home by ten o'clock, stopped off at the pub for a beer with his cronies, and time just slipped away. He dragged in at 2 a.m. He slipped out of his shoes, sneaked up the stairs, headed for the bedroom where he knew his wife had been for hours, with a tight grip on his shoes so he wouldn't drop them and awaken her.

As he passed the coo-coo clock, it opened its big mouth and coo-cooed two times. Thinking very sharply for a man full of brew, he loudly coo-cooed eight more times. He listened and hearing nothing from the bedroom, he proceeded to undress and slipped into bed. He smiled and mentally patted himself on the back for such a brilliant maneuver, then slumbered off.

The next morning at breakfast his wife said: "I want you to get that coo-coo clock repaired." And he asked: "Why, what's wrong with it?" And she shot back, looking him squarely in the eyes: "Well, this morning I heard it coo-coo two times...hiccup...burp...flatulate...then coo-coo eight more times!"

KEEPER MEMORY Bill Moore was the best all-around angler/shooter I've known in a lifetime of associating with some fine ones. This Texan always had a droll tale to tell each time we met.

He went to a friend's ranch for a morning of quail hunting. The foreman was a character named Ephriam, Eph for short, and he loved to coon hunt. He'd gone through several blue tick hounds over the years Bill had known him, and now he had the latest one he had been training for several months. Bill probed: "Want to show him to me?" Eph said: "Follow me, he's out behind the barn."

On the way out Eph told Bill all about the blue tick's fine blood lines...about how big and strong he was...how he ate more than two normal coon hounds...what unusual markings he had...and what a great watch dog he was. As they rounded the barn corner, there laid the big hound, sound asleep, head inverted, and lips curled showing stained teeth. His feet were twitching, and he was obviously dreaming he was on a hot trail. "Really, Eph, what kind of coon dog is he? Eph sighed: "Mistuh Bill...to tell the truth, he's doin' his damndest right now!"

• • • • • • • • • • • • • • • • •

TWO OLD HUNTERS were in their turkey blind, giving an occasional "Elp, elp!" on slate calls, trying to lure an old tom close enough for a shot. Unknown to them an equally old, anti-hunting gal thought she would spoil their chances for success. She stripped off all her clothes and streaked toward their blind.

As she sped past, both hunters squinted, and one asked: "What the heck was that ol' gal wearin'?"

The other old hunter replied: "Dunno, but whatever it was sure needs pressin'!"

THE YOUNG BOY SCOUT was on his first overnight camping trip, thrilled at the chance to pass three merit badge tests: hiking, tracking, and cooking. Upon returning home his dad asked what they had cooked. He replied: "A piece of steak, potatoes, and carrots stuck on a stick and cooked over a fire. And the scoutmaster said to pass we had to cook it, eat it, and not throw up!"

ANOTHER VERY OLD, in his 90s, outdoorsman was proud of his fitness at his ripe old age. And to prove it to himself he entered the foyer of a dating service and told the receptionist: "I want the fastest gal you got for an evening on the town. Know what I mean?" She replied: "Sure do. Just sit down and I'll call Edna. She's just your type."

The old man sat down in an easy chair and promptly fell into a snoring sleep. Edna came, heard his request, gave him a gentle wake-up tap, smiled and said: "Old timer, I think you've had it. He replied: "I did? Well, I sure hope I enjoyed it!"

● ● ● ● ● ● ● ● ● ● ● ● ● ● ● ● ● ●

THE SUNDAY SCHOOL TEACHER was telling the kid class what a marvelous feat Noah accomplished in building the ark to make it accommodate two of each animals on earth. During the Q & A period, one youngster asked: "What do you suppose they ate for 40 days and 40 nights? They couldn't eat any of the animals."

Another youngster replied: "Probably took along a lot of fruit."

"Naw," another answered: "That stuff spoils fast."

Still another replied: "Why I betcha I know. They were afloat, so they caught and ate a lot of fish."

A young fisherman in the group shot back: "Are you kiddin'...on two worms?"

● ● ● ● ● ● ● ● ● ● ● ● ● ● ● ● ● ●

HIS FISHING BUDDY smoked like a wet fire and he tried everything he could think of to get him to quit. Then, one day he tried some psychology on him.

"Good buddy," he said. "Smoking those fags will kill you. Now I've watched you sit in a boat for ten hours without a nibble, and never blink an eye. Anyone with that much willpower can quit smoking. All you need is a substitute habit pattern, and I've got one for you. Here, carry this box of toothpicks with you. Whenever you feel the urge to smoke, just pop a toothpick into your mouth and chew on it until the urge is gone."

Sure enough, it worked...his fishing buddy began chewing on toothpicks and quit smoking... but he died of Dutch elm disease!

• • • • • • • • • • • • • • • • •

MOTHER TO LITTLE SON: "The pastor's going fishing and I promised to pack his lunch. Deliver this sack to his home so he can take it with him."

The pastor thanked the little boy, looked over the lunch and said: "Yummy, especially that small, fresh apple pie. I'll be sure to thank her for that." And the little boy said: "Sir, would you mind thanking her for two apple pies?"

• • • • • • • • • • • • • • • • •

HE TRAVELED THROUGH Virginia to fish its lovely flowing waters but pampered his wife by yielding a day to take her to some lovely, old colonial shops.

Everything she expressed a liking for he found some kind of fault with so she wouldn't buy it. In one classy antique store, she fell in love with an early American brass poster bed with a canopy. The salesman gave a nice rundown on its authenticity, winding up with: "As a matter of fact, both Julius Caesar and George Washington slept in this bed."

And the fisherman snorted: "Aw, come on now. How could they both have possibly slept in this bed?"

The salesman smiled and said softly: "Well, as you observe, it's a double bed."

And his wife chided: "See, smart ass!"

THE AVID BASS FISHERMAN tried to impress his companion by relating that blue is the number one seller in plastic worm colors, and that no one knows why.

"I know why, it's the only color bass can feel," replied his sharp buddy.

"What do you mean they 'feel' it?" he snorted.

And the answer came back: "Man, haven't you ever felt blue?"

• • • • • • • • • • • • • • • • •

HE HAD BEEN FISHING all day and was heading for home, skunked, whitewashed, and feeling lower than whale dung in a submarine track. Then, he suddenly grinned, and turned into the fish market. He looked into the display case, pointed, and said: "Let me have six of those bluegills, and don't wrap them. Just put them in a plastic bag."

The clerk did so, the man paid him, then walked about six paces away. "Now, please toss me that bag of fish," he requested. The puzzled clerk did so, but said: "I don't understand."

The fisherman caught the bag of fish and replied: "Well, I may be a lousy fisherman but I'm not a damned liar. Now I can honestly say I caught them!"

• • • • • • • • • • • • • • • • •

THE BIG FISHERMAN married a midget, four-foot tall wife. Every time he took her fishing she complained of pain in both her groins.

On the way home he stopped by the family doctor's office. The doc examined her, fumbled around, and said: "Now try walking."

She replied: "The pain is all gone, what did you do?"

Doc replied: "I just cut off the tops of your husband's knee boots you've been wearing fishing!"

KEEPER MEMORY I was conducting a seminar at the Zebco plant with several hundred members of the Tulsa Bass Club in attendance. They were an avid audience, eager to hear about whatever tactics might help them outsmart more bass. I mentioned that tests show a bass has the ability to remember.

One big, ol' boy said: "Okay Uncle Homer, got a question. My buddy and I were fishing stickups, both using the same color plastic worm. I got a hit, set the hook, fought a bass for several minutes, it leaped, then busted my line and took off. He cast the same color worm to the same stickup, got a hit, set the hook, and finally landed his bass. It had my worm sticking in the corner of its mouth. Now, if as you say a bass can remember, why did it hit the same color worm so soon after it got hooked on one?"

I replied: "A bass has two memory centers, one for each eye. Let's say its left eye saw your worm but its right eye saw your buddy's worm. You see, the right eye memory center would have no recall of having been hooked before."

That big, ol' boy stared at me and drawled: "I knew I shouldn't have asked the damned question in the first place!"

• • • • • • • • • • • • • • • • • •

THE TOWN GRAVE DIGGER was good. He could look at a casket and dig a hole that fit like a glove. But when the town giant died, a former basketball star almost eight feet tall, he got his first big challenge.

He began digging late in the day and still was shoveling dirt when it got too dark to see. So, he called it a day and tried to jump up to grab the rim so he could climb out. He had dug the hole just too deep, so after several tries he knew he couldn't make it, so he sat down and dozed off.

A coon hunter was following his hound on a trail through the cemetery, couldn't see, and fell into the big hole. He began jumping up, trying to grasp the rim, when the grave digger awakened. He could barely make out the outline of the coon hunter as he kept jumping upwards. So the digger eased up behind the coon hunter, tapped him on the shoulder, and said: "You can't get out of of here that way." But, he did!

● ● ● ● ● ● ● ● ● ● ● ● ● ● ● ● ●

AROUND OUR NATION there are two common ilks of fishermen who never get skunked. Those who never go bass fishing, and those who lie about it!

● ● ● ● ● ● ● ● ● ● ● ● ● ● ● ● ●

FISHERMAN'S PRAYER God grant that I may fish until my dying day...And when at last I've come to rest I'll then most humbly pray...When in His landing net I lie in final sleep...That in His mercy I'll be judged...As good enough to keep!

● ● ● ● ● ● ● ● ● ● ● ● ● ● ● ● ●

THE FISHERMAN noticed activity on a distant shore, so he rowed his boat close.

A young man was giving mouth-to-mouth resuscitation to his companion at the water's edge. The young man was holding the victim's mouth open and sucking water out of it. He would spit out the water, then suck out another mouthful. This went on for quite some time, and the young man was obviously growing weary from the exertion. He looked up at the observing fisherman and asked: "I'm doing this just like I learned in Red Cross first aid, but I must be doing something wrong. Got any suggestions?"

"Yep," replied the fishermen. "If you don't pull that man's fanny out of the water...you just might suck this lake dry!"

THE BIG, BURLY outdoorsman had an achy tooth and the one thing he hated most in the world was going to a dentist. But since it might cut into his hunting and fishing, he went. He settled down in the chair and as the dentist walked up, the B.B.O. reached down and grabbed the dentist where it wasn't nice, gently but firmly.

The dentist looked at him curiously and asked: "And just what are you doing that for?"

The B.B.O. gave him a one-sided smirk and drawled: "We aren't agonna hurt each other, are we doc?"

• • • • • • • • • • • • • • • • •

JOHN HICKS, a young reporter from Des Moines, was interviewing Irvin S. Cobb, noted writer and humorist who had a very sharp tongue. The interview took place in Cobb's spacious suite in downtown New York City.

All went well until Cobb began to get a little bored. He looked at the reporter and said: "John Hicks, hey? Well, young man, here you are in one of the world's largest and busiest metropolises. Do you know what happens to 'hicks' in New York?"

And John Hicks came back: "No, but I know what happens to 'cobs' in Iowa." *(for "city folks"...corn cobs were a substitute for toilet tissue!)*

• • • • • • • • • • • • • • • • •

THE EDITOR OF the New York Daily News became friends with the editor of the London Times at an international peace conference. They agreed to keep in touch, read each other's papers and offer any helpful suggestions which came to mind.

The New York editor noted an article in the Times which read: "A shooting affray took place in Cafferty's downtown pub, and during the melee a young woman was wounded by a gunshot. At presstime, the bullet was in her yet." The New

York editor cut out the article, and couldn't refrain from blue-penciling in the margin "Pray tell...where is her 'yet'."

And the Times editor wrote back: "Yes, our idioms undoubtedly sound a bit odd to you Yanks at times...but, then, so do some of yours seem peculiar to us. To answer your question, it is in the same vein as that old American ballad of yore: 'I wonder who's kissing her now.'"

●●●●●●●●●●●●●●●●●●

TOM MANN, noted bass angler, looked over his audience eager to hear about their favorite fish. He grinned and said: "I feel like a mosquito in a nudist camp. There is so much territory to be covered, I'm not sure where to begin!"

●●●●●●●●●●●●●●●●●

KEEPER MEMORY A lot of memories were made during my developing years when I enjoyed 16 of these working my way up the ranks at Heddon, then the world's largest lure maker.

Many of these came from my close association with Lou Caine, president, who took this young aspirant from Ohio and taught me much about coping in a very competitive business. Just before attending my first industry meeting, he said: "Make notes of the names of those individuals who get on their feet and do the most talking...and those company execs who do the least talking but say something of value when they do. When you return to the office, look up their ratings in Dun and Bradstreet. The talkers will have the lowest ratings...the sayers the highest in our industry."

He was right! Then there was the time when some industry mag was doing an article on Lou, and evidently needed to know his age, which he never revealed. The wire was tersely worded: HOW OLD LOU CAINE? And Lou wired back: OLD LOU CAINE FINE, HOW YOU?

64

THE CANNIBAL CHIEF was hosting supper for his favorite hunting and fishing buddy. Word had spread that the chief's mother-in-law had just passed away. The buddy, a man who spoke his mind, helped himself from the stew pot and said: "You know I couldn't stand much of your mother-in-law." The chief replied: "So, just eat the noodles!"

65

TWO NUNS ran out of gas on a country road and remembered they had passed a country store a short piece back. But they didn't have a container to carry gas in.

One nun chuckled and said: "I think I have a solution. I just happen to have a bed pan in the trunk. It will hold enough to get us back to the store for a fillup. The good Lord doth provide!"

So she took the bed pan to the country store while the other stayed with the car. She had just returned with the "gas pan" and they were pouring it in the tank when two men in a camper drove past v-e-r-y s-l-o-w-l-y.

The driver ogled the two nuns and said to his companion: "See that there, fella...now that's what I call a real test of faith!"

• • • • • • • • • • • • • • • • • •

A FISHERMAN in a small rowboat was fishing in a fog. Out of nowhere a big cruiser emerged and banged into him. No real damage was done and the confused skipper tried to back off but instead banged into the little boat again.

"Can you stay afloat?" the skipper bellowed through his megaphone?"

The fisherman replied: "Guess so. Why, are you gonna try again?"

• • • • • • • • • • • • • • • • • •

KEEPER MEMORY I was wading and fishing for bass along the shore of Ohio's Indian Lake when I came upon an elderly person seated in a folding chair. Two crutches revealed a mobility problem.

He smiled and asked: "Catchin' any?" And I gave the usual defensive reply: "Not yet, but I just now got started. Do you fish?" "Oh yes, every day," he replied. "I've only been out an hour and have three nice catfish for supper. All channels, see?"

And he pulled in a stringer with three beauts around two pounds each. Seeing none, I asked: "Where's your fishing gear?" "I use my 'power line,'" he replied, "see here."

He reached down and picked up a heavy cord tied to his chair leg. Hand over hand he coiled the cord between his legs. Then, out of the water came two hooks baited with liver. "See," he pointed, "there's my bait."

Then, to my surprise, as he paid out line the bait was mysteriously pulled back into the water. He explained: "My son ties a long rubber strip to a rock which he plants about 50 feet from shore. Then he ties my line to the rubber strip. So, it 'powers' the bait in and out without my having to cast." Pretty canny, eh?

● ● ● ● ● ● ● ● ● ● ● ● ● ● ● ● ● ●

SPLATTERPOLIN'   On my first trip to Florida in the late '40s, I was bass fishing with Tom Denmark in a lake near Orlando. We were laying plugs about every three feet along a cypress-kneed shore, but the bass weren't responding. We detoured around an old black gentleman who nodded/smiled to thank us.

Just as we began pulling away, I noticed him pick up a long cane pole and begin beating the bejazus out of the water surface with that pole. I thought he was showing his exasperation at catching no fish and mentioned it to Tom. And Tom replied: "Nope, he's splatterpole fishin', something you'll never see up north because it's a native lore.

"You see, he's speck fishing, you call them crappies. When he hasn't had a bite he figures he's fishing where the specks ain't. So, he beats the water to make a noise like a school of feeding specks. A passing school hears this and comes in to get in on the gorging. Watch him, hear?" He baited up two poles and in exactly five minutes he began catching crappies two at a time. It won't work every time, but it's worth trying!

YARN SPINNING is all a part of hunting camp evenings. One of these sessions was in full sway and one oldtimer was telling his annual ferocious grizzly story.

"Yep, I hunted all morning, got hungry, set my rifle against a tree, unpacked my lunch and began eating. I dozed off, was awakened by a deafening roar, and saw a giant grizzly rushing at me, teeth slavering and eyes glaring.

"Well, I didn't have time to grab my rifle, so I looked overhead and the nearest limb was ten feet high. So, I made a leap for it just as that grizzly made his final leap at me." Then he paused for dramatic effect.

"Well, obviously you must have reached the limb or you wouldn't be here telling about it," one of the group observed, dryly.

"No, actually, I missed the limb," he replied.

"Well, if you missed that damned limb then how could you possibly be here today?" the doubter continued.

And the yarn spinner replied: "Well, you see, I did miss the limb when I jumped but I got it on the way down!"

• • • • • • • • • • • • • • • • •

KEEPER MEMORY During one of our ten trips to Alaska, we met a petroleum engineer who shared some memorable moments with us.

He told about camping on an island, and the river came up so much at night they had to evacuate. His two companions tried to wade ashore but their clothes filled with heavy volcanic silt and both drowned. He clung to a tree all night and waited until the river receded the next day.

Deciding he needed some R & R, he took a week to go hunting for a Kodiak grizzly...a trip he'd dreamed about for years. The guide sat him down by a big tree and said:

"I'm going to fan out and make a lot of noise down trail. Usually, the bear will move away from human sounds and come your way. So, keep alert and watch the trail."

The engineer sat down, rifle across his knees, noticed a brown hump about 50 feet away, but paid it no attention. He dozed off, heard a loud roar, turned, and saw an awesome grizzly standing erect whuffing at him. He concluded: "One mile later, I stopped running and realized I had left my gun with the grizzly!" Now, this is one Alaskan bear story I could envision, and believe!

•••••••••••••••••

CHRIST AND ST. PETER went bass fishing on a heavenly lake. The Lord peered in his tackle box and selected his favorite perch-finish plug. He made one cast, began reeling, reared back to set the hook...fought hard...and brought in a 60-pound largemouth bass.

"Not bad," observed St. Peter. "That's almost three times the world record."

So, he reached into his tackle box, pulled out his favorite crank bait, made a long cast and had barely began reeling when he grunted, set the hook, and battled in a humongous bass. It tipped the scales at 75 pounds! The Lord winked at him and said:

"Ummm, Pete, let's cut out the miracles and just fish, okay?"

•••••••••••••••••

LITTLE BOY asks his buddy: "Notice all those circles with the BB mark smackdab in the center? All those are Butch's with his initials, and they are all over the neighborhood. I draw circles and shoot purty good but I can't get 'em dead center like Butch. How do you suppose he ever got to be so super-accurate?"

And his buddy replied: "Easy, I watched him. Butch shoots first and then draws the circle!"

PUN-ISHMENT Once upon a time there was a renowned sturgeon on the staff of this health fishility. A reel, fin fellow, he was one of its flounders. He was wiser than salmon and never shrimped from his responsibilities. He was always up-scale and whistled a happy tuna.

One day a young patient, a mere whipper snapper, told the sturgeon his medical theories were full of abalone. He trouted all over town saying the sturgeon's medicine had made him more eel than he was before, and conched the sturgeon with a mal-practice suit.

The board demanded his oyster, and he was in a real pickerel. But because the case smelt to the high heaven, the wise old judge finally denied the plaintiff clam...whereupon the board tried to hire the sturgeon back. But, alas, because of the pressures he had been under, the old sturgeon had been hitting the bottlenose very hard. As a matter of fact, it brings us to the end of our shad tale, because the sturgeon finally wound up on squid roe. Buoy...ain't that a fine kettle of guess what?

● ● ● ● ● ● ● ● ● ● ● ● ● ● ● ● ●

MORE PUN-ISHMENT The young man came to the priest and said: "Father, I must put more of myself into church than I have been. May I call people to mass Sunday, my way?" "Be my guest, my son, if it will fulfill you," the priest replied.

Sunday morning he climbed into the belfry, put his hands behind his back, and used his head to "BONG!" the big bell. Three times be bonged and with the third he fell into the area-way, deader than a dornick.

People crowded around as the priest walked up. "Who is this young man?" they asked. "Well," he replied, "I don't know his name but his face rings a bell." Monday morning a young man walked up to the priest and said: "Do I look familiar, Father?" "Why, yes," he replied, "just like the young man who made a supreme sacrifice last Sunday." "Well, I'm his twin brother, and I won't be able to rest unless I carry on his mission. May I call the people to church Sunday, Father, my way?'' The priest replied: ''If it will put your soul at ease, my son, be my guest!''

Pre-mass time came Sunday morn and the young man climbed into the high belfry. With both hands behind his back he stuck his head inside the big bell, and ''BONG...BONG...and the third BONG, he fell, splattt, into the areaway, deader than the mackerel he ate the night before.

A crowd gathered around and the priest walked up to gaze down at the sad sight. ''Who is this young man, Father?'' someone asked. And the priest replied: ''Well, I don't know his name...but he is a dead ringer for the young man who was here last Sunday.'' (There, I have carried this horrible two-gun pun around long enough. Now it is yours to carry!)

•••••••••••••••••••

THAT DALMATIAN DOG which firemen always seem to take along with them, according to all we hear and see? There are varied opinions as to why. One school of thought says that this spotted critter is used to bark crowds backwards to keep them away from a fire. Another declares it is taken along for good luck. But, anyone who knows anything about dogs knows firemen take a dog along for one purpose...just to locate the nearest fire plug!

•••••••••••••••••••

KEEPER MEMORY Joe Godfrey established one of the early Fishing Halls of Fame. At the banquet when John Alden Knight was to be inaugurated, Joe asked me to make the presentation. I had never met John until that occasion, but I thought it would be novel to do it with a different flare.

''Before I make this well-deserved award to the father of the Solunar Tables, let me tell you how it all began. John had made friends with a bounty hunter who always got game and caught fish. They were having a drink together, and John

71

asked him what was his secret. As he talked about his 'moon under' theory, John made notes on the white table cloth. When the man finished, John smiled and said: 'You know, I believe I can sell this theory. But I've got to think up a name for it.'" The scofflaw said: 'That's easy. Where are we?' John replied: 'Why, in a saloon.' 'And what're you writing on?' the bountyman pursued. 'On a table,' John observed. '"Well, there's your name, saloon-er table!' quipped the canny character." The audience laughed, but John just raised a bushy eyebrow!

● ● ● ● ● ● ● ● ● ● ● ● ● ● ● ● ●

A FISHERMAN who was caught with ten more bass than the law allowed was taken to court by the conservation officer. The judge fined him heavily, and asked: "Do you have anything to say?" Yes, your Honor," replied the fisherman. "I surely would appreciate six copies of the court record to show my bassin' buddies!"

● ● ● ● ● ● ● ● ● ● ● ● ● ● ● ● ●

DO YOU SUPPOSE the time will come when computers will become sufficiently programmed to demand at least two "circuit breaks" a day...or they'll go out on strike?

● ● ● ● ● ● ● ● ● ● ● ● ● ● ● ● ●

DRESSED IN CAP AND GOWN after his graduation from college, the young man handed his diploma to his father and said: "Well, I finally managed to finish law school to please you and mom. Now I'm going to become a professional bass fisherman like I've been insisting since I was old enough to watch Bill Dance's TV show!"

WHATCHOO THINK Elmer? Is it gonna clear or not?

THE AVID HUNTER/ANGLER charged with deserting his wife stood before the stern-looking judge who had just pronounced him guilty. "Your honor," he said. "If you knew my wife you wouldn't call me a deserter...you'd call me a refugee!"

• • • • • • • • • • • • • • • • •

FOUR FARM KIDS in high school played hooky to go "crick fishing" one spring morning. They returned in time to attend afternoon classes and explained to the teacher that the aging pickup had a flat tire on the way to school. To their surprise she just smiled very nicely and said: "Well, you boys missed a test this morning, so I'm going to give you another one. Each of you take a corner seat and get out your pencil and paper. All ready? Okay, each of you write an answer to this question. Which of the four tires was the flat one?"

• • • • • • • • • • • • • • • • •

THEY WERE PLAYING poker in the Deadman Saloon when the dealer suddenly stood up, pulled his .45, and laid it on the table. "This game is crooked, by dingydongies...and Ah'n agonna let daylight through the next man who cheats!" The bartender who had been watching the play asked: "Now why would you make such a serious accusation as that, Deadeye?" And Deadeye replied: "Because that feller a-sittin' across from me played a different hand than the one I dealt him!"

• • • • • • • • • • • • • • • • •

KEEPER MEMORY Shortly after we moved to Arkansas, I met Slim Keck whose fame had preceded him. I had heard his family had the best recipe for country-cure hams. We became friends and quail-hunting buddies and were sipping coffee one morning before setting out. I said: "Slim, I know your family ham-cure recipe is confidential, but can you show me where you cure them?" "You betcha," he replied, and motioned for me to follow.

He took me out to a three-holer biffy sitting behind the house. "People who don't know us think we haven't got inside plumbing. But I bought this outhouse new and all it's been used for is curing hams. You raise the rear cleanout lid to build a smoking fire and hang the hams inside to cure. The three holes let the smoke rise to fill the inside and the half moon in the door lets it out slowly. We have had several strangers passing by knock on our front door to tell us our outhouse was on fire. We allus thank 'em and tell 'em grandpa just got a new corncob pipe and was out there breakin' it in. They allus walk away lookin' puzzled, but we have had nary a ham stolen."

• • • • • • • • • • • • • • • • •

I LEARNED TO LOVE native humor because of its colorful tang. Here are typical Arkansawyer stories I heard during our ten-year stay in that state where part of our hearts always will remain.

Two fishin' buddies were getting ready to leave for their weekly catfishin' effort when one looked out in the pasture and said: "Hey, where did you get the cow?"

"I bought her at an auction so we could enjoy some fresh, un-store-bought milk," he replied.

And his buddy observed: "I notice she's a-lyin' down. I've heard it said when cattle are a-lyin' down during the day it's a bad time to go fishin' because all wild critters will be doin' nuthin, and doin' it real slow. You believe that?"

"Well, let's don't take any chances," he came back. He strolled over, kicked the cow in the fanny to get her on her feet, climbed back in the pickup and said: "Now, let's go catch some fish!"

WE STOPPED along a busy highway to buy fruit at a stand. My Arkansas friend watching all the cars whiz past opined: "Lookit all them dang fools rushin' to git some place where they'll be overly sorry to see them when they git there!"

• • • • • • • • • • • • • • • • •

THE CENSUS TAKER was working his way through the Ozark hills when he knocked on the door of a little cabin. A buxom hillbilly gal opened the door with a smile and he asked if he could come in to ask his survey questions. She said: "Shore, come right in!" showing him to a well-worn easy chair while she sat down on a rumply davenport.

As they talked he simply could not keep his eyes off her lovely pair of bosoms. Suddenly in ran a big, tow-headed boy weighing about 120 pounds. He whispered something in her ear and she shook her head negatively. He again whispered, this time more animatedly. She sighed, unzipped her blouse, and handed him one.

The census taker was aghast, and asked: "M'am, is that your son?"

"Yup," she replied.

"Well, how old is he?, the man pursued.

"Fourteen," she replied.

"Well, have you ever tried weaning him?" asked the amazed and envious census taker.

She sighed and replied: "Shore have, but he throws rocks at me!"

• • • • • • • • • • • • • • • • •

THE GAME WARDEN heard through the grapevine that a certain scofflaw had been bringing home a tubfull of fish every time he went fishing. So, he made a date to go fishing with the suspect. After they arrived in a nice, little cove the warden said:

"Now, show me how you've been getting a tubfull of fish every time you go, Johnboy." So, Johnboy reached into his rucksack, pulled out a stick of dynamite, lit it, and handed it to the warden. The warden looked at the sputtering fuse, gasped and said: "Don't you know this is against the law?" And Johnboy said: "You gonna sit there and just talk or you gonna fish?"

• • • • • • • • • • • • • • • •

THE OUTDOOR EDITOR went fishing with Jeb Blodget for a how-to story. Jeb caught a small bass and before he "put the little feller back" he reached into his tackle box and pulled out a pint of bourbon. He poured a drop in the little bass's mouth, then turned it loose.

"Why?" asked the writer.

"Well, little bass are blabbermouths. They go home and tell the big bass not to bite on our lures, and they won't. But when a kid bass comes home and blabs with booze on his breath, no big bass is gonna believe a word it says!"

• • • • • • • • • • • • • • • •

KEEPER MEMORY Sam Walton was my quail hunting buddy in Rogers, AR where he founded his first Wal-Mart store in 1962. In January of '63 we let our birddogs out of his pickup in a likely looking field and there was about two inches of snow on the ground. I glanced down and noticed his little toe pushing his sock out through a hole in his boot.

"Sam," I observed, "you've got a whole new store with lots of boots to choose from...why wear a boot with a hole in it?"

And Sam replied: "Uncle Homer, if there's one thing I hate worse than a cold toe...it's breaking in a new pair of boots!" God no doubt could have made a better hunting buddy and an American who gave more of himself to his country than Sam Walton. But no doubt God never did!

77

WHILE FISHING with Larry Lazoen, one of the nation's better pro bass anglers, I asked him: "I know you make a full time living fishing bass tournaments. How often are you home and do you have a family?"

"I'm home about three days a month, and have a wife and two kids," he replied. I pursued: "Well, is your wife happy?" And Larry answered: "About three days a month!" Pro bass fishermen are a special breed who need very special wives to keep the homefires burning!

● ● ● ● ● ● ● ● ● ● ● ● ● ● ● ● ● ●

KEEPER MEMORY: Way back in the early 1930's right after graduating from Springfield (Ohio) High School, I began working in Reco Sporting Goods store. One of my responsibilities was running their fishing contest. It was my job to measure, weigh, and record data on what, where, and when the fish was caught. So, I got fairly good at estimating the weight of a fish on sight.

One Saturday afternoon a southerner brought in a largemouth bass. As he held it up for all to see, I mentally said...about 6 1/4 pounds. When I put it on the scale the needle settled on 7 1/2 pounds. I thought...no way!

I upended the fish, shoved my cupped fingers down its gullet, popped open the throat, and began shaking the bass up and down as I inverted it over a glasstop counter. Immediately, lead shot began pouring out of the bass's mouth and splatting off the glass surface.

I glanced up at the angler's face with lips which held a soggy cigar butt. He daintily removed it with thumb and forefinger, gave me a mirthless grin and drawled: "Bass sho' do eat funny things, don't they?"

THE ORVIS COMPANY from day one produced some of the world's finest fly rods and was the first to impregnate bamboo with bakelite. This innovation eliminated mildew which made the six sections come apart, and the rod taking a set, both derived from the inadequacies of animal glue. This was because the founder, Charles Orvis, was both a pioneer and a perfectionist. He had his booth arrayed with his superb fly rods at the Boston Sport Show and was there to proudly display his wares. A local strolled in, picked up a top grade fly rod by its middle, shook it so that both ends wobbled crazily, and asked in his Bostonian drawl: "What kinda pole is this?" Charles Orvis looked him squarely in the eyes and replied crisply: "Young man...God makes poles...Orvis makes rods!"

• • • • • • • • • • • • • • • • •

KEEPER MEMORY: After a quarter century of marriage and shaving, I decided to grow a moustache while away on a two week trip. My Childbride met me at the airport, kissed me sweetly, spotted the hairy lip, and whispered in my ear: "I know the second thing you're gonna do when we get home!"

• • • • • • • • • • • • • • • • •

KEEPER MEMORY: One of our travels for world wide fishing articles took us to Holland where we stayed at the Amsterdam Hilton. We made a date with a cab-driver fisherman to take us around to good holes he knew in the area.

I was attired in a jumpsuit, as usual, and just happened to pick a gold color for the day. I went down to check on things while Childbride finished preening. As I stood by the front door waiting for our driver, a little, old English lady came up to me and said: "Young fellow, would you please help me with my satchels?"

I smiled and said: "Be happy to, m'am!" I picked up her three bags and nestled them into her compact car. She thanked me, opened up a snap-top purse, fished around and came out with a dime which she plopped into the palm of my hand. I thanked her kindly and as I entered the hotel I noticed that the bellhops also were wearing gold jumpsuits. Then I knew why she had approached me for help, and chuckled.

At that moment Childbride appeared, saw the coin in my hand, and said: "What's the dime for?" I replied: "From a nice, little old lady who made me feel needed!"

● ● ● ● ● ● ● ● ● ● ● ● ● ● ● ● ● ●

ERNIE PYLE, revered war correspondent, once wrote: "Writing a daily column is a whole lot like fishing. You throw your fingers onto the typewriter keys and hope you'll catch a stringer full of words. But, sometimes the words just aren't biting!"

● ● ● ● ● ● ● ● ● ● ● ● ● ● ● ● ●

THE BIG SUPER-JET was enroute to a distant airport, and flew over a small lake in the pilot's home bailiwick. He pointed and said to the co-pilot: "See that small lake down there between those two hills? When I was a kid I'd sit down there in a boat, fishing for bluegills. And every time I saw a plane fly over, I'd look up and dream I was piloting it. Now, I look down and dream I'm fishing for bluegills!"

● ● ● ● ● ● ● ● ● ● ● ● ● ● ● ● ●

WIFE SHOWING HUBBY a new, very expensive fur coat she just bought: "I can't help but feel sorry for the poor critter that was skinned for this!" Husband: "Thanks, I appreciate your sympathy!"

THIS IS RANDOLPH, the rude nosed reindeer. He could run just as fast as Rudolph...but he couldn't stop as quickly.

KEEPER MEMORY: Back in the mid 40's when I arrived in Dowagiac, MI to begin my career with Heddon Fishing Tackle, the hotel was filled and the clerk recommended I call on Emily to see if she had a spare room. She did not, but it was a cold, snowy night and she invited me in to sit a spell, while she popped corn and served warm cider.

It was a very nice evening and as I was departing she paused at the door to say: "Young man, as you begin your new career, there will be times when the load is too heavy and sleep won't come. I'm going to share with you a prayer which you won't forget, and I'm going to tell it to you just one time. 'Lord, when upon my bed I lie...sleepless... unto thee I'll cry. When my brain has worked o'er much...stay the wheels with thy soft touch. Just a loving thought of Thee, and Thy tender mercy. Just a little prayer, and then...I shall go to sleep again.'"

I didn't forget. I'm glad to share it with you. Remember it. And I truly believe it will lighten your load, as it has for me, when it's so heavy that sleep is elusive.

• • • • • • • • • • • • • • • • •

FISHERMAN to school superintendent: "I got home too late to attend the PTA meeting, but my name is Harry James and I'm curious to know if my wife got up to speak last night?" Superintendent: "I don't know your wife but there was one lady who said she just couldn't find words to express her feelings." Fisherman: "Hmnn, sure wasn't my wife!"

• • • • • • • • • • • • • • • • •

A WISE, OLD INDIAN CHIEF sent a message to the president of the United States, advising: "I suggest you revise your immigration laws and make them far stricter than ours were!"

DOC: "You told me your arthritis was so bad you couldn't hunt or fish any more. I took time to treat you, and you gave me a check which came back. What do you have to say?" Fisherman: "No problem. The arthritis came back, too!"

• • • • • • • • • • • • • • • • • •

KEEPER MEMORY: When I am teaching a class of kids about fishing and the fascinating outdoors which surrounds it, I share with them this poem written many years ago by Aleta McPherson:

"When you walk through woods I want you to see, the floating gold of a bumblebee; rivers of sunlight, pools of jade, toadstools resting in mossy jade. A cobweb net with a catch of dew, treetop cones against the blue, dancing flowers, bright green flies, and birds, to put rainbows in your eyes.

When you walk through woods, I want you to hear a million sounds that await your ear; the scratch and rattle of wind-tossed trees, A rush!...as a timid chipmunk flees. The cry of a hawk from the distant sky, the purr of leaves as a breeze sweeps by. Brooks that murmur, rocks that ring, and birds to teach your heart how to sing.

When you walk through woods I want you to feel that no mere man could make this real...

Could paint the throb of a butterfly's wing, nor teach a wood thrush how to sing; could fashion the wonders of earth and sky; ah yes, there's something far greater than you or I. When you walk through woods and the birches nod...pause...meet a friend of ours... His name is...God!"

And as you savor these sapient words, remember when the load gets overly heavy and you just can't carry it alone...your great outdoor father is never more than a prayer away. Find a quiet, arboreal spot and ask Him to lighten the burden you've been bearing. He will. I know. He has lightened mine many times over 78 years!

WHEN WE MOVED TO ARKANSAS I was fascinated by native lore. I soaked it up like a sponge, curing my own country hams with local recipes, finding bee trees for honey gathering, etc.

Then, I tried to make persimmon beer and ran into a problem. When we went to church my wife noticed a couple of gnats buzzing around my head. They followed me out to our car. I went home and took a hot shower plus a thorough scrubbing.

After arriving at work monday morning, my secretary, Reba, a native Arkansawyer, strolled into my office for the usual conference. She tipped her head sideways, smiled, and observed:

"I bet you've been making persimmon beer!"

"How in the world do you know that?" I asked. Reba replied:

"Well, grandad used to make it and after every batch the gnats followed him around for a couple of days, too!"

• • • • • • • • • • • • • • • • • •

HAVING BEEN HAPPILY HITCHED to one lady for 56 years, I'm expert enough to believe: there are no homely gals, some just prettier than others...no fat ones,some are just wider for their height. And for every woman who has made a fool out of a man, there are a thousand women who have made a man out of a fool.

• • • • • • • • • • • • • • • • • •

KEEPER MEMORY: When I was sports editor on the Springfield (Ohio) News Sun, I had great hours. Worked Wednesday through Saturday, then off until the next Wednesday...but I worked two shifts on Saturday, from 5 a.m. to 2 a.m. Sunday.

About 3 a.m. I arrived home and took my usual shower, being careful not to awaken Childbride. I had a full head of hair and to tame it I had made a cap out of an old nylon hose. I failed to find it in its usual place, so I sought a substitute.

In her sewing cabinet I found an old brassiere with elastic between the two cups. I placed this over my hair and knotted the ties under my chin. It worked nicely, so I climbed into bed. At daybreak I began dreaming that a bat was diving on me...could even hear its wings flapping together. I sat up in bed, flailing my arms at that danged bat, quite comatose. I felt a tap on my shoulder and heard Childbride say: "Just what in hell are you doing?" When it dawned on me that all she knew was her husband was sitting up in bed, brassiere cups over his ears, beating the air like mad...I replied with dignity: "Somehow, I don't think it's any of your danged business!"

• • • • • • • • • • • • • • • • •

A DOG WARDEN in a small town received a call from a mature maiden lady who said: "I wish you would come out here and remove these ten dogs which are milling around, panting, tongues lolling, and creating pandemonium in my flower garden." And the dog warden said: "Well, m'am, do any of them look mad?" There was a pause and she measuredly replied: "Well, I'd say eight of them have a good reason to be!"

• • • • • • • • • • • • • • • • •

LITTLE WIFIE: "Now, let's see. You caught 63 pounds of assorted fish last year. I've kept tab on all your trips and what with gas, oil, fishing tackle, torn pants, repairs and such, those fish cost you $22 a pound, dearie."
Fisherman: "Okay, dearie. Let's get out the check stubs for the past 18 years and see what you've cost by the pound!"

NEWS ITEM IN A SMALLTOWN NEWSPAPER: Lottie Primrose was granted a divorce from her husband, Zekie, champion tournament fisherman. She sued on grounds that he had spoken to her only three times in the past three years. She was granted custody of their three children.

● ● ● ● ● ● ● ● ● ● ● ● ● ● ● ● ●

A SUNDAY MORNING fisherman had just started rowing away from the dock when a guy rushed down the gangway and shouted: "Hey, Wilbur, your house is on fire!"...then ran back up the gangway. The fisherman hurried madly back to the dock, dashed to his car, and roared homeward. Suddenly he slammed on the brakes and muttered: "Whatinell am I hurrying home for...my name isn't Wilbur?!"

● ● ● ● ● ● ● ● ● ● ● ● ● ● ● ● ●

THE TWO FISHING buddies met at the dock at crack of dawn, Sunday morning. One looked like he had a horrible hangover, nose red, bags under his eyes, and sagged like an old potato sack. His buddy said: "Hey, how you doin'?...you look great!" The sot retorted, sourly: "Well, I wish I could say the same about you." His buddy replied: "You could if you were as big a liar as I am!"

● ● ● ● ● ● ● ● ● ● ● ● ● ● ● ● ●

I CHOOSE TO BELIEVE...that the good Lord, being a fisher of men, designed fishing with especial detail. He must have decided that men, women, and kids should go fishing, and that they should catch fish, but not always. There will be days when we catch fish, and some days when we get whitewashed. After all, isn't it the blank days which make the good days seem all the sweeter?

OUTDOORSMAN'S PRAYER Lord, as I older grow, grant me these things... The ability to be conversational, but not long-winded. Grace enough to be compassionately attentive to others' tales of aches and pains...but let me quietly abide my own miseries, lest they increase as retelling them grows hauntingly sweeter.

Quiet my craving to straighten out other people's affairs. Show me how to measure outdoor pleasure in nature's blessings, not in creel or bag limits.

Help me to approach serious things lightly and light things seriously. Remind me regularly that my liveliest opinion might be dead wrong.

Make me ever thoughtful, never moody; gently helpful rather than commanding. Let me laugh at my gaffs and inadequacies so that when others do it, no hurt results. Help me to give each hour of every day the utmost effort with the talents you have given me. Teach me to strive for excellence, not drive for perfection...knowing I will fail part of the time and must learn to live with my average. And, when the last, long cast is ended, dear God, may you be pleased with what my soul has caught!

•••••••••••••••••

HUMAN NATURE A young man paused to chat with an old man he met at the outskirts of a town he visited for the first time.

"What kind of people do you have in this town, old man?" he asked.

"What kind did you find in the town you just left?" asked the old gentleman. And the young man replied: "A real bunch of cornballs...unfriendly, stingy, and really hard to get along with."

"Well," said the oldster, "that's about the same kind of people you'll find in our town." Later, another young man approached the town and paused to visit with the old man.

"Pardon me, sir, I'm new here. Would you be kind enough to tell me what kind of folks I'll find in this town."

"Son," replied the old man, "what kind did you leave behind you?" And the young man replied: "Some of the finest folks in the world...kind and generous, very friendly and honest. I'll miss them in many ways."

"Son," replied the elder gentleman, "you'll find the same kind of fine, kind, generous, friendly, and honest folks in this town. I bid you welcome!"

• • • • • • • • • • • • • • • • •

THE GIRL'S FATHER had a date to go fishing the next morning at crack of dawn, but his daughter's boyfriend lingered in the parlor past midnight, and showed no signs of leaving. Her father strolled into the parlor and asked the young man:

"I'm curious...what would you do if you suddenly came into some money?"

"The young man thought, smiled, and replied: "No doubt about it, I'd travel."

"Good thinking, my boy," replied the girl's father, and handed him a dime.

• • • • • • • • • • • • • • • • •

WHITE TUNA were first harvested commercially many years after pink tuna had become the most popular canned fish. The marketers were having a hard time getting housewives to buy white tuna so they hired a public relations agency to help them get a larger share of this market. It was a good move because the canny agency team made up attention-getting stickers which they applied to all the canned white tuna in the warehouse, reading: WHITE TUNA, GUARANTEED NOT TO TURN PINK IN THE CAN!

TWO OLD HOUND DOGS were returning home after a long coon chase. They passed by a lawn fete where a bunch of young folks were dancing to the beat of a hard rock stereo. They watched the gyrations for some time, and the older hound dog commented: "Y'know, when we act like that they give us a worm powder!"

WHY DO I FISH? There are almost as many answers as there are fishermen. Here is mine.

Over 65 memorable years I have pursued outdoor trails amidst nature's grandeur accompanied by selfless men whose friendships I treasure. Men who put more into the sport than they ask in return...men who look to the comfort of others first, themselves last.

Why do these men go beyond the pale of usual fishing to endure unnecessary hardships in their favorite sport of fishing? Some will tell you it's the whopper they hope to catch. In the beginning this may be so, but this is an elusive quest which soon fades with the years. Here are motives I've seen.

*To be a kid again and laugh with other adult kids, if only for a few hours, to shed the shackles of regimentation.

*To meditate, to daydream, to watch woes and aches run down a line to get lost in a mystic, challenging creature called a fish.

*To commune with nature, reverently in God's great, green cathedral...a fallen log for a pew, the songs of birds for a choir, and towering trees whispering a sermon for those with ears to hear.

*To endure pangs of discomfort as you drive yourself to keep going in cold rain or foul weather. The weak turn back, the true seeker presses on, urging forth those mysterious extra reserves nature gave us but we so seldom use.

*To purge our soul of petty thoughts which obsess us in the mad scramble today for prestige, power, or self, whatever the motive. Out there in the bigness of the outdoors, small people don't endure, and demeaning thoughts are replaced by benevolent ones.

*To learn the laws of survival by observing wild creatures. We must be careful in our planning because Mother Nature is coldly unforgiving of shallow thinking. There are places where to forget is to perish.

*To learn skills and crafts that carry through from youthful into the elderly years, giving rich pleasures throughout a lifetime.

*To teach my family, plus other kids and oldsters, and give all within reach opportunities to enjoy this priceless heritage, fishing, when it is denied to so many others in our harried world!

● ● ● ● ● ● ● ● ● ● ● ● ● ● ● ● ●

A BUS LOADED with a tour group was listening to the driver describe points of interest as they cruised a scenic highway. Here's how it went. "See that sprawling mansion on the hill over there? Now that's the home of John Rockefeller."

Little old lady in back seat: "Is that John D. Rockefeller, the oil man?"

"No, lady," replied the bus driver, "it's John Rockefeller, the big man who played tight end for the Oilers." A little farther on: "You see that three-story castle over there? Well, that's the home of Henry Ford."

Little old lady: "Is that Henry Ford, the pioneer auto maker?" Reply: "No, lady, that's Henry Ford, the rock star noted for dirty lyrics."

A couple miles farther: "Now that big place all in white and covering about two acres...that's the Church of Christ." There was a pronounced silence. Then a wag in front of the bus turned his face toward the rear and sang out: "Go ahead, lady, ask him. You can't be wrong all day!"

● ● ● ● ● ● ● ● ● ● ● ● ● ● ● ● ●

A DISGUSTED ANGLER who took the Chicago el from the loop to Evanston to fish off the north piers wrote the company: "For the past 18 months I have been riding your el, the service seems to get worse every day. I think the transportation you offer today is worse than people had 10,000 years ago! I've had to stand up every trip." Signed: John "Aching Feet" Jones.

And a "cute" PR man at the transit authority wrote back: "We received your letter of the first, and believe you are somewhat confused in your history. The only transportation ten thousand years ago was by foot!'' Signed: Charles Smartie.

''Aching Feet'' Jones replied: ''Methinks you are the one who is confused in your knowledge of ancient history. If you will read the bible, the Book of David, you will find where Aaron rode into town each day...on his ass. And that, Mister Smartie, is something I haven't been able to do on your el for the past 18 months!''

• • • • • • • • • • • • • • • • • •

TAKE YOUR BOY FISHING What is the gift you would give your boy? A glamorous game, a tinseled toy, a whittling knife, a puzzle to pick, a computor game with fancy stick, a Boy Scout book, a real live pet, no, plenty of time for these things yet. Give him a day for his very own, a walk in the woods, a game in the park, a fishing trip from dawn to dark. Give him the gift that only you can, the companionship of ''his old man.'' Games are outgrown, and toys decay, but he'll never forget... if you give him a day!

• • • • • • • • • • • • • • • • • •

PRUNELLA PINECOAN was hauled before the local magistrate for shooting her husband with a bow and arrow. The judge knew the family well, and he asked, puzzledly: ''Prunella, I know for a fact that you're pretty good with a rifle and have one on your mantle. Why in the world did you shoot Zekie with a bow and arrow?'' And Prunella replied: ''Wal, it were late at night and I didn't want to woken up the kiddies!''

DIDJAKNOWTHIS: Tree leaves give off great amounts of water, like a medium-size maple tree sweats as many as 50 gallons of water daily. This is why trees shed their leaves in winter. Otherwise they would die of dehydration.

• • • • • • • • • • • • • • • • •

TWO WILD CANARIES were winging south on their annual migration. Suddenly the male's head whipped backwards as he stared at something on the ground. He said: "You go on ahead, I just saw something back there that need's checking!" He plunged downward while she flew slowly on. About 15 minutes later he caught up with her and he was a sad-looking mass of frazzled feathers. "What in the world happened to you?" she asked. And the male canary replied: "Guess I'll have to be a little more discerning. I just got caught up in a really wild badminton game!"

• • • • • • • • • • • • • • • • •

FATHER WAS BREAKING SON into the sporting goods business. He stressed that he must listen to dad to see how he made sales, wrapped packages, made correct change, exhuded courtesy, and made the customer feel important.

One customer was in a hurry, bought $35 worth and handed dad a $50 bill. He grabbed his change and hurried off. After he was gone, dad said to son: "Look, two $50 bills were stuck together. Now this brings up a question of ethics and honesty. Should I tell my business partner or not?"

93

THE ANGLER HAD just hauled in a whopper trout when a "tree hugger type" happened to be strolling along the stream. As he grabbed it to put in his creel, she gasped: "Oh, the poor thing, how can you possibly kill it?" And the angler replied: "Lady, if it had kept its big mouth shut it wouldn't have gotten into trouble!"

● ● ● ● ● ● ● ● ● ● ● ● ● ● ● ● ● ●

THIS SAME TYPE of protester showed up at a conservation club meeting during the deer hunting season. A biologist was explaining why they were having an open season on doe deer, mostly because of over population and many deer would starve. She took over the mike and protested vehemently against "the killing of mother deer." After about a five minute tirade she sat down. The biologist smiled and asked her if she ate meat. She replied of course she did, but she didn't go around killing animals, and if she were a hunter she certainly wouldn't kill the mothers of any species because they were meant to bear young. The biologist smiled and asked: "When you buy pork chops, do you question the butcher about the sex of the animal?"

● ● ● ● ● ● ● ● ● ● ● ● ● ● ● ● ●

GOOD NEWS/BAD NEWS STORY His wife strolled up to his easy chair where he was reading the daily paper. "Honey," she said sweetly, "I've got some good news and bad news."

"Give me the good news first, maybe it will help me through the bad." "Nope," she came back, "I'll give both at the same time. You know that new all-terrain pickup you're so proud of? Well, the air bag works beautifully!"

THERE ARE THREE REASONS for the persistence of fishermen. One: fish are biting; two: fish are not biting: three: they might turn on. Any one of these is rationale for always arriving home late!

• • • • • • • • • • • • • • • • •

A PESSIMIST is any fisherman who thinks the weather is too foul to catch any fish. An optimist is any wife who thinks he won't try anyhow.

• • • • • • • • • • • • • • • • •

DIDJAKNOW: Blacksmith are forgers from way back; dachshund owners keep a low profile; schools of fish sometimes play hooky; light bulbs never know watts happening; window washing is a pane; senior citizens like elderberry wine; chimney sweeps have a lot of flue; raising rabbits is a hairbrained idea; and most women believe all bigmouth bass are males while smallmouth bass are females.

• • • • • • • • • • • • • • • • •

IT WAS SPRING, the ice had just melted from the lakes, and Zekie was heading out the door with his fishing tackle. He paused, glanced over his shoulder, and drawled: "Marthy, is there anything important you want to say before the fishing season starts?"

• • • • • • • • • • • • • • • • •

TO MAINTAIN a happy marriage, you must drink the lucid cup. When you are wrong, admit it, but when you're right, shut up!

THE FAMILY DROVE into the campground and the four kids jumped from the car, began unloading the gear, put up the tent, and worked feverishly gathering firewood. Then they all disappeared. A nearby camper marveled at such teamwork, and asked the father how he managed such discipline. He replied: "Well, I have a rule. No one goes to the bathroom until camp has been set up!"

• • • • • • • • • • • • • • • • • •

AN OLDSTER went to the doctor's office to have his blood pressure checked. The office was crowded and he sat so long his legs fell asleep. When the nurse finally called him he limped into the examining room. A few minutes later he walked briskly out. One old patient nudged another and said: "Dunno what the doc charges, but he must be worth it!"

• • • • • • • • • • • • • • • • • •

OLD ADDAGE: "A fool and his money are soon parted." Today, it happens to everyone!

• • • • • • • • • • • • • • • • • •

THE OLD MAN stood at the latrine, patiently waiting for it to happen. While he stood there, a young boy rushed up to the next stall, unzipped, tinkled quickly, zipped, and started to dash away. At that moment the old man's water happened, and two streams came out. The little boy stopped, fascinated by what he saw, and said: "Mister, do you always pee two streams?" The old man smiled, and replied: "No, son...only when I'm in a hurry!"

"I DON'T CARE who you say you are, fat boy... just get those stinkin' animals off my new roof!"

THE OLD LADY phoned the emergency fire number and shouted: "FIRE, FIRE...my house is on fire. How fast can you get here!" The excited chief replied: "Well tell me how do I get there?" And the old lady shot back: "Why in that big, damn, noisy red truck, you old fool!"...and hung up!

● ● ● ● ● ● ● ● ● ● ● ● ● ● ● ● ● ●

THE WOMAN AND MAN were engaging in a little hankypanky when they heard a car drive up. The woman said:

"Oh, that's my husband. Quick, hide in the closet!" So the man darted into the closet and closed the door. He heard a small voice say:

"Sure is dark in here, isn't it?" And the man whispered: "Quiet, kid, don't talk!"

"Wanna hear me blow a bugle?" the kid whispered. And the man replied:

"Heck, no, now be quiet, hear?" The kid whispered: "Give me 20 bucks or I'll blow the bugle."

"Here's a 20, now be quiet!" the man said.

"Wanna hear me beat a drum?"

"Okay, I know, here's another 20, now be quiet, dammit!" They heard the car drive off and the man darted away. The little boy came out holding two 20's and his mother asked where he got them.

"From the man who came into the closet where I was checking on my Christmas gifts you hide there," the boy replied. And his mother said: "Now you know that's wrong and if you want any Christmas gifts you've got to go right down to church and confess, or you won't get a thing. Do I make myself clear?"

The little boy shook his head and took off. He eased into the confessional, closed the door, and remarked: "It sure is dark in here, isn't it?" And a voice next door came back: "Now don't start that crap all over again, kid!"

T'WAS THE SEASON TO BE JOLLY and the Salvation Army crews were out doing their thing. The captain and his aide went back to headquarters after a long day. The captain took his shower first, and as he came out to dry off, the aide chuckled and said: "I swear, you've got the ugliest navel I've ever seen!" And the captain came back: "Okay, wise guy, tomorrow you carry the flag!"

• • • • • • • • • • • • • • • • • •

HE GOT BORED lying in the hospital bed, waiting for the doctor, so he thought he'd have a little fun with the new, young nurse. He hid his morning grapefruit juice and later poured it into the urinc-sample bottle. When she picked it up she quipped: "My, a little cloudy today, aren't we?" He said: "Let me see that." She handed it to him, he held it up to the light, squinted, and said: "Shore is, let's run 'er through again!" He gulped it down. The nurse fainted!

• • • • • • • • • • • • • • • • • •

THE LITTLE OLD LADY came her first day to do housework for the madam. She hung her hat on the hatrack and placed a brown bag below on the floor. As she dusted she saw a box of chocolates, got the brown bag, and purloined the top layer. Later, madam went for a chocolate, saw the top layer missing, noted the brown bag, looked inside, saw the chocolates, and promptly put them back in the box. Later the little old lady looked in her brown bag, saw it was empty, put on her hat, and left, snorting: "I don't work for no one what steals back!"

IN A SMALL SOUTHERN TOWN this little gal was strolling around in her new, stretch pants at the local carnival. A pickpocket saw the impression of her pocketbook through the right pocket of her tight pants. He eased up in a crowd and deftly used his shiv to remove the pocket and pocketbook in one easy maneuver.

Unaware, she moved on and met her friend who promptly remarked: "My, my, but you do look nice in those new, stretch pants. I bet you like 'em!" "Oh yes, I do, because besides being the latest style, they're so handy. Lookee...I keep my comb in this pocket, my lipstick in this pocket, my change in this pocket and (feeling into the now departed pocket) in this pocket I keep my steel wool...uh...steel wool? I don't carry no steel wool!"

• • • • • • • • • • • • • • • • • •

HILLBILLY PAPPY: "Whatchoo teachin' mah son in school, when he could be doin' chores at home?" Teacher: "We teach him history, spelling, English, and trigonometry." Pappy: "Wal, bear down on that triggernomitty, hear? He's the sorriest shot in the whole family!"

• • • • • • • • • • • • • • • • • •

A THUNDERBOOMER STORM was raging outside and when the mother tucked in her little boy said: "Mama, can I sleep with you tonight?" And she replied, gently: "I'm really sorry but, you see, I have to sleep in daddy's room with him." After a long silence with heavy breathing, his quavery little voice remarked: "Well, okay, but what makes daddy such a big sissy?"

A RICH MAN reached the pearly gates and St. Peter asked: "What have you done to deserve entering the kingdom of heaven?"

"Well," replied the rich man, "let me cite all my good deeds. I met a decrepit woman and gave her two cents to help her plight. Then, I met a begger who was hungry, and I gave him two cents. And just yesterday I met a newsboy on the corner who was shivering from the cold, and I tipped him a penny. I try to be aware of the other person's needs and share my wealth accordingly."

St. Peter turned to Gabriel and said: "Gabe, you heard the man. What do you think we should do with him?" And Gabriel replied: "Give him back his nickel and tell him where to go!"

• • • • • • • • • • • • • • • • •

WEATHERCAST First it blew, then it snew, Next it friz, then it thew, Soon there came a shower of rain, Then it friz and thew again. Out came the sun, a lovaley thing, Thinking it threw, then I knew Snew, friz, and thew meant spring!

• • • • • • • • • • • • • • • • •

NEWSBOY: "Extra! Extra! Two men hornswoggled! Customer: "Here boy, I'll take a paper!...why there's nothing in here about two men being hornswoggled!" Newsboy: "Extra! Extra! Three men hornswoggled!"

• • • • • • • • • • • • • • • • •

A NUT AT the wheel, a peach at his right, A curve in the road, fruit salad tonight!

THE HOBBY of a successful business man was his flower garden. One day he came home early and was out making things beautiful. A reserved lady in a party dress stopped her car when she observed his lovely yard, saying:

"My good man, do you have any free days to work for me. I need a good yard man." He replied: "No, madam, not at the present."

And she replied: "But, I'll be glad to pay you more than you're making here."

He winked and whispered: "It isn't just the money...you see, I get to sleep with the lady here!"

• • • • • • • • • • • • • • • • •

THE OLD BUFFALO hunter was found after he had been ambushed by hostile Indians, lying beside his dead horse, scalped, and barely breathing, yet smiling. The wagon train scout propped him against the dead horse's saddle, gave him a drink of water, and asked: "Does it hurt, podnuh? And the old hunter responded: "Only when I laugh!"

• • • • • • • • • • • • • • • • •

HE STOOD ON the crowded elevator with a big, delighted smile growing on his face as more passengers got on and pushed tighter against him a sweet, young chick standing in front of him. With each floor his smile grew and so did the scowl on the face of his wife who was taking it all in. When the elevator stopped on the main floor, the young chick suddenly turned, bopped him on the head with her purse and said: "I'll teach you not to pinch me!" Embarassed, he turned to his wife and said: "I did not pinch that young lady, I swear!" And his wife consolingly replied: "I know, I did!"

PUZZLE   The lady mounted a city bus and the driver charged her full fare for her son who was wearing long pants. At the next corner a small boy wearing short pants was charged only half fare. At the next stop a sweet, young lady headed for a nudist camp was charged nothing. Why? She had a transfer!

• • • • • • • • • • • • • • • • • •

SAM BOUGHT a new retriever called a Heavenly Hunter. He took his buddy duck hunting, shot a mallard, told the dog "Fetch!"...and the dog took off, tippy-toed over the water surface, picked up the duck, and tippy-toed back, dry as a bone. The shooting, commands, tippy-toeing, and retrieving took place until they had a limit. Sam said: "Notice anything unusual about my new duck dog?" "Yeah," replied his buddy, "the damned dog can't even swim!"

• • • • • • • • • • • • • • • • • •

IN YOUR GRANDPA'S day, people used to look at a baby and ask: "Is it a boy or a girl." Today they ask the same question about college seniors!

• • • • • • • • • • • • • • • • • •

ZEKIE CLAGGHORN says: "One advantage of being poor: car keys never are in your other pants...and everybody is endowed with life, liberty, and the national debt.

A TEXAS HUNTER stopped at one of those pay-to-hunt farms in Oklahoma, and the farmer was justly proud of his 500-acre farm. "Is this your entire farm?" the Texan asked. "Why back in Texas I get in my car at daybreak and drive all day. At dusk I arrive at the other end of my ranch." The farmer smiled and replied: "Yep I know, I used to have a clunker like that!"

• • • • • • • • • • • • • • • • •

DIDJAHEAR ABOUT the young Indian who went to college and became an electrical engineer. To show appreciation to his tribe for paying his tuition, he set up a small power plant to provide power for the reservation. He also ran a line to the outhouse so they could see in the dark.. It was the first time in history that an Indian wired a head for a reservation.

• • • • • • • • • • • • • • • • •

IN THOSE FISHING CAMPS where you give up good dollars for bad quarters...wouldn't it be a neater idea if they had square bathtubs? Sure it would, then they wouldn't all have rings around them.

• • • • • • • • • • • • • • • • •

WHAT HAS SIX BOWED legs, two heads, smells bad, has two manes, wears six worn-out shoes, and would rather "git a long little dogie" than git a short little dogie? A cowboy on an old cayuse.

"I NOW PRONOUNCE you husband and wife...uh...would one of you please kiss the bride?"

GLEN: "I hear your wife got one of those expensive mud packs on her face last week. How did it work out?" Gary: "Well, she looked greatly improved for about three days, then the mud fell off."

• • • • • • • • • • • • • • • • •

FISHERMAN: "Doc, this danged toothache comes and goes but lately it comes just as I am about to go fishing. You might as well pull the danged thing out but, first, tell me how much it costs." Doc: "Thirty five bucks." Fisherman: "You guys are getting worse than plumbers...$35 for about two minutes work is way too high! Is there any other choice?" Doc: "Well, if you'd like it better, I can extract the tooth v-e-r-y s-l-o-w-l-y!"

• • • • • • • • • • • • • • • • •

TWO KIDS IN VERBAL HASSLE, first kid: "My father is better than your father!" Second kid: "Ain't not!" First kid: "My brother is better than your brother!" Second kid: "Ain't not!" First kid: "My mother is better than your mother!" Second kid: "Well, now, I guess you've got me there. My dad says the same thing!"

• • • • • • • • • • • • • • • • •

WOMAN: "Are you the kid who jumped into the river and saved my kid from drowning when he fell through the ice?" Kid: "Yes ma'am." Woman: "Well, where are his hat and mittens?"

ONE PEDIGREED DOG said to the other: "Oh, here comes that unpedigreed mutt, and they say he has the coldest nose in town. Quickly, sit down! They sat, and the mutt strolled up, saying: "Oh, uh, hi there ladies...uh...what are your names?" One snooty lady dog said: "Why, my name is Fifi, spelled F..I..F..I." And the other snooty lady dog replied: "And my name is Mimi, spelled M..I..M..I. And, pray tell, just what is your name?" The mutt thought a minute, then replied: "Why, uh, oh yeah, my name is Fido... spelled...P..H..I..D..E..A..U..X!"

PRO TO FLANAGAN: "I know you're in fine fettle and want to learn golf in a hurry, but it is a very demanding game. You see that little hole way down there with the flag? Just hit it in that direction."

Flanagan blasted a powerful drive and when they went to see where it landed, it was resting one inch from the rim of the cup. "Tremendous," said the pro. "The idea is to get the ball in the cup with the least number of strokes." Flanagan snorted: "Now you tell me!"

•••••••••••••••••

AFTER THE CLASS REUNION which his wife couldn't attend because she had the flu, she asked: "Did you see your old girl friend, Sally Klotch? "Yep, I sure did. And she should be very good in investments," he opined. Wife: "Because she's kept her girlish figure?" Hubby: "Kept it? She darn near doubled it!"

•••••••••••••••••

THE OLD PROF teaching physiology liked to shock each new freshman class into reality. So, he began by holding in his left hand a bottle of liquid with a floating object, and shouting: "STUDENTS...in my hand I hold a diseased male organ!"

It always served its purpose and got their attention quickly. But, in this particular class he happened to have an itch in his crotch, so he reached into his pocket to scratch it...just as he said he had a diseased male organ in his hand. One sharp freshman quipped: "Okay, but whatcha got in the bottle, Doc?"

THE TELEPHONE RANG and the woman asked: "How you feeling?" She replied: "Miserable. Got a splitting headache, sick at my tummy, the house is a mess, and the kids are driving me crazy!" Woman: "Tell you what. You go lie down and I'll come over, cook lunch, clean the house, and look after the kids for you. By the way, has my husband picked up Sam to go fishing yet?" She replied: "There's no 'Sam' here...you must have dialed the wrong number...but I hope that doesn't mean you aren't coming over!"

• • • • • • • • • • • • • • • • • •

YOUNG REPORTER: "You're a remarkable 105-year oldster, and I'd like to hear how you reached this amazing age?" Old man: "Well, it's clean livin', pure thinkin', married to the same gal for 70 years, and daily exercisin'." Reporter: "What kind of breakfast do you prefer to kick off with each day?" Old man: "Well, I can't rightly answer that question yet. You see, I'm dickerin' with three cereal companies for the highest bidder!"

• • • • • • • • • • • • • • • • • •

HAT DEFINITION: What a man seldom wears any more...a beggar passes around...a statesman tosses in the ring...a wife blows her whole allowance on...a politician talks through...and a fisherman never throws away!

• • • • • • • • • • • • • • • • • •

FISHERMAN: "What do you mean...nightcrawlers now cost a buck a dozen? Why Clark's bait store has them for 50 cents a dozen." Bait store man: "Then why didn't you buy them there?" Fisherman: "Because he was out." Bait store owner: "Why that robber! When I'm out I sell them for 20 cents a dozen!

A POACHER and a game warden were boyhood friends. The poacher learned his wayward ways from his backwoods family and lived by his wits. The game warden had gone to college and enjoyed his profession because he loved the outdoors. Off duty, they were friends.

One night they were having a beer together and the warden said: "Let's play guessing games like when we were kids. Every time we miss we pay a dollar." The poacher said: "Now wait a dadburned minute. You bin to college, I ain't. When you miss you pay a dollar and when I miss I pay 50 cents." The warden agreed, and the poacher asked the first riddle: "What has six legs, eight eyes, has no wings but flies around at night?" The warden didn't know and gave the poacher a dollar. The poacher didn't know either so he paid the warden 50 cents.

• • • • • • • • • • • • • • • • • •

ONE MOTHER: "I just can't get our son out of bed in the morning without a big hassle. How do you do it?" Other mother: "Simple. I just toss our big cat into bed with him" One mother: "How does that help?" Other mother: "He sleeps with his bulldog!"

• • • • • • • • • • • • • • • • • •

LIFEGUARD TO HOTEL GUEST: "Sir, I've been watching you for the past three evenings after you leave the bar...and you simply must stop urinating in the pool." Guest: "Why heck, every one pees in the pool, you know that." Lifeguard: "Yes, I know, but not from the diving board!"

THE 75-YEAR-OLD WOMAN visited her family doctor and begged him to give her a prescription for birth control pills so she could get some sleep. Her doc said they wouldn't do a thing to help her sleep, but she insisted they would. To humor the old lady he went along and wrote the prescription for a month's supply of birth control pills.

About a month later she was back and said: "Oh, doctor, those pills worked great, I've slept soundly all month. But, now I need another prescription." Doc: "Look, Mrs. Smith, I'm a physician and I know there's nothing in those pills which will help you get to sleep...unless it's simply your imagination."

The old lady replied: "You're a doctor, I'm a grandmother who has an 18-year-old granddaughter living with me. Every morning I've been sneaking a pill in her orange juice. Believe me, I surely sleep better!"

• • • • • • • • • • • • • • • • •

I'M AN OCTOGENARIAN, my life has been spent, My get-up-and-go has got up and went, but, oh, how I grin...when I think where it's been!

• • • • • • • • • • • • • • • • •

KEEPER MEMORY Bodie McDowell, cherished buddy and founder of the Outdoor Writers Scholarship Fund, and I were riding in the bed of a pickup on a Texas game ranch. We were there to observe and shoot pictures, not animals.

The driver stopped so we could look at a herd of kudus, the African animal with long, spiral horns. As we watched I gave Bodie a stick of gum and began peeling one for myself. Bodie nudged me and said: "Unc, look behind you!" Almost as tall as we was a cow kudu with neck and head extended toward me, sniffing. "I think she wants some gum, too," said Bodie. So, I offered the stick I had peeled and she took it.

I began peeling another stick for myself when suddenly I felt my butt gently hoisted off the edge of the pickup bed. Bodie observed: "I think she's trying to tell you she wants another stick of gum." I handed it to her and again, she gently took it from my fingers. Bodie chuckled, saying: "You know something, you may have made a bit of history today. You're probably the only outdoor writer ever to be goosed by a kudu!"

• • • • • • • • • • • • • • • • • •

KEEPER MEMORY: We were on a Braniff Outdoor Council jaunt to the Galapagos Islands and my companion for the day was Lew Klewer, veteran outdoor writer with the Toledo Blade. We were traveling light with just cameras, and a thermos of iced tea Lew carried because there was no water on the island.

After a couple of hours hiking around to observe giant turtles, sea lions, and other wildlife, we hunkered down for a cold drink. Lew handed me a cup, then began pouring his own. Out of nowhere came a mocking bird which perched on the rim of his cup and began drinking. She sat there, unafraid, and kept dipping her beak into the cup.

Lew's bristly moustache curved upward in a big smile as he squinted one eye and commented: "Over many years I have shared drinks with a lot of fine, feathered ladies, but I'll say one thing. You're one of the daintiest and purtiest!" I have that picture in my file and cherish it!

• • • • • • • • • • • • • • • • •

TIMES HAVE CHANGED: Young man to his date's mother: "Excuse me for coming to the door, but the horn on my car isn't working."

1ST BOY SCOUT: "How do you tell toadstools from mushrooms?"

2ND BOY SCOUT: "Eat some before you go to bed. If you wake up in the morning, they're mushrooms."

MOST MEMORABLE FISHING TRIP: This is a hard choice but because of unusual aspects, a trek to Ecuador's Andes mountains to catch hybrid cutthroat/rainbow trout with retired Colonel Sam Hogan gets the nod.

At 10,000 feet, Wally Taber and I unloaded our cameras and fishing gear. We climbed a slippery slope then slid down the other side to a ledge which overlooked a lovely lake in a deep valley. "How do we get down?" I asked. Colonel Sam pointed to the top of a 75-foot tree about three feet from the stone ledge.

"We climb down that tree," Sam smiled.

"You go first and show us how," I grinned. With gear draped over his neck he fell into the tree and began shinnying down. We followed and spent a delightful day catching six- to ten-pound beauties. Sleet, snow, and rain came with intervals of sun when we shot pictures. All the time we fished, the thought recured: "How do we get back on that ledge?"

When the time came I followed one of the agile guides. In addition to cooking gear he had two big trout inside a poncho draped over his head. He climbed to the top of the tree and began swaying. As if spring-released he vaulted onto the rock ledge and held onto some dry grass. He unloaded his gear, turned to me with arm extended and said: "Venga!" (Come!)

We grasped each other's wrist and he literally yanked me onto the ledge. With my free hand I grabbed hold of his pigtail and held on. We both wound up laughing like a pair of idiots, carried away by the moment. And it was a moment of accomplishment...a keeper memory!

● ● ● ● ● ● ● ● ● ● ● ● ● ● ● ● ●

YOU NEVER CAN DO a kindness too soon...because you never know how soon it will be too late!

THE DRAFT DODGER was asked by his friend: "How'd you manage to get a 4F rating? You are in perfect health." And the DD replied: "I showed the doc the truss I had on and he said that made me a 4F."

His friend paid him a buck and borrowed his truss. He put it on and went to the same doc for his physical. The doc examined him and asked: "How long you been wearing this truss?" And the young man replied: "Why, uh, about nine years."

The doc shot back: "I'm recommending they send you to Egypt." "EGYPT!" the young man exclaimed, "but why?"

And the doc replied: "Well, I figure anyone who can wear a truss upside down for nine years would have no trouble riding a camel."

● ● ● ● ● ● ● ● ● ● ● ● ● ● ● ● ● ●

KEEPER MEMORY: We were filming the Sports Afield TV series in North Carolina, in Roland Martin's old stomping grounds, and my segment was finished. Glen Lau, the producer, said: "If you want to go bass fishing while I finish up with Roland, enjoy!"

I was like a kid at recess. I took off in my waders, belly box full of lures, and using 20-pound mono line I flipped a plastic worm over a ledge and felt a bass suck it in. I wasted no time setting the hook, saw a whopper leap high amidst a burst of water...then suddenly the line went slack. Knowing the bass either got off or was swimming toward me, I reeled like mad to catch up with the bass just as I felt it dash between my legs and wrap around both my ankles! There I stood, hogtied by a big, mama bass. I tried breaking the line, found it impossible, so I whipped out my handy sheath knife, stooped down as waders filled with water, and cut the line. As I stood there soggy from head to toes, that lunker bass leaped not six feet away, and shook her head as if to say: "Soooo long, sucker!" A cherished image in a 65-year fishing montage!

115

ONE OF THE HARDEST disciplines we try to convey to grandkids is to teach them that the secret of learning to save money is to spend what you have left each week after the saving...instead of saving each week what's left after the spending.

• • • • • • • • • • • • • • • • •

BOY SCOUT CAMP was over and one kid was seen rumpling up his pajamas and squeezing out half a tube of toothpaste onto the ground. "Why are you doing that?" asked his tentmate. And he replied: "Just to please mom and see her smile!"

• • • • • • • • • • • • • • • • •

YOUNG CAMPER, wringing out soggy blanket, "Does your tent always leak like this?" Old camper: "Heck no, only when it rains!" Young camper: "Is it true that an alligator won't grab you if you are carrying a lantern?" Old camper: "Depends on how fast you are carrying it." Young camper: "While you were out fishing today I thought I'd surprise you so I stayed in camp and baked you an apple pie. But the dog ate it." Old camper: "Oh, that's okay...he was gettin' purty old anyhow." Young camper: "You know, you have an amazing waistline?" Old camper: "Why do you say that?" Young camper: "If a Douglas fir was that big around it would be 60 feet tall."

• • • • • • • • • • • • • • • • •

EVERYONE IS ABLE to give a measure of pleasure to someone. By taking your fishing buddy to a newly discovered hotspot you've found. By leaving it to the angler who is there when you arrive!

ONE GUY: "Would you believe a burglar got into our house about two o'clock this morning, just before I got home from fishing?" Other guy: "Did he get anything?" One guy: "Yeah, the poor guy's in the hospital with a concussion. My wife thought it was me!"

•••••••••••••••••

REPORTER TO ASTRONAUT: "As you sit there just before takeoff, strapped in your seat, waiting for the big blast that will take you and several million dollars worth of instrumentation into outer space for a week, how do you feel?" Astronaut: "How would you feel if you were sitting atop 15,000 parts which you knew were supplied by the lowest bidders?"

•••••••••••••••••

A BIG, BURLY truck driver was eating his breakfast in a roadside diner. Eight raunchy motorgangers voomed up, parked in a row, and came inside. The leader clomped over to the truck driver and put his cigar out in the driver's eggs. Another gang member doused his cigarette in the driver's coffee. The driver arose, paid his bill, walked out to his 16-wheeler, and roared off in a cloud of dust. The gang leader said to the waitress: "Not much of a man, that driver." And the waitress replied: "Not much of a driver, either, he just ran over eight motorcycles!"

•••••••••••••••••

WIFE: "You don't love me any more, you don't seem to notice that I'm around. I bet you don't even remember the day of our marriage!" Angler: "Oh, come on, of course I do. It was the day I got up real early, sneaked out fishin', and caught my first ten pound bass!"

117

THERE WAS this little girl, she was ten, going on eleven. Now that girl is thirty eight, says she's going on twenty seven.

● ● ● ● ● ● ● ● ● ● ● ● ● ● ● ● ●

"YOU MEAN TO TELL ME you're going to spend your two weeks vacation camping way out in the wilderness in a tent? I don't see how in the world you can keep yourself busy."

Camper: "Neither do I. That's why I go camping way out in the wilderness in a tent!"

● ● ● ● ● ● ● ● ● ● ● ● ● ● ● ● ●

VETERAN CAMPER to son: "I've never seen anyone ask so many questions about the outdoors. I can't help wonder what my father would have thought if I had continuously fired questions at him." Son: "Maybe if you had, you'd be able to answer more of mine."

● ● ● ● ● ● ● ● ● ● ● ● ● ● ● ● ●

SMALL BOY, as he watched his parents come home from the hospital with triplets. "Oh boy, we'd better put a big ad in the paper...these are gonna be a lot harder to get rid of than that last litter our cat had!"

● ● ● ● ● ● ● ● ● ● ● ● ● ● ● ● ●

ZEKIE CLAGGHORN allowed as how if someone had just invented the safety pin today it would have a transistorized spring with a variable switch for weak fingers...and iffin it breaks, don't even think about having it repaired. It's a whole lot cheaper to just throw it away and buy a new one.

EVER HEAR WHERE the limbo dance really originated? It was in Scotland right after they put in the first dime pay toilets.

THIRTY DAYS hath September, April, June and November, according to my coachin'. Thirty days also hath a hunter feller I know...serves him right for poachin'!

• • • • • • • • • • • • • • • • •

WHEN I HEAR olden, melodic music I try to picture the person who composed it. When I hear today's hard rock I have no trouble picturing the person who decomposed it!

• • • • • • • • • • • • • • • • •

THE OLD FELLER visited the specialist who fitted him with his invisible hearing aid. He thanked him and related how much he had been enjoying it. "I bet your family likes it too," observed the specialist. The old feller chuckled and replied: "They don't even know I've got it... and I enjoy listening to their chats when they don't know it. Already I've changed my will several times!"

• • • • • • • • • • • • • • • • •

ZEKIE CLAGGHORN saw all the traffic coming toward him and decided he must be late because everyone else was coming back. He was driving the wrong way on a one-way street!

• • • • • • • • • • • • • • • • •

WOMAN TO MARRIAGE COUNSELOR: "That's my side of the situation. Now let me tell you his."

BASS SERIES LIBRARY
by Larry Larsen

(BSL1) FOLLOW THE FORAGE - BASS/PREY RELATIONSHIP - Learn how to determine dominant forage in a body of water and catch more bass!

(BSL2) VOL. 2 BETTER BASS ANGLING TECHNIQUES - Learn why one lure or bait is more successful than others and how to use each lure under varying conditions.

(BSL3) BASS PRO STRATEGIES - Professional fishermen know how changes in pH, water level, temperature and color affect bass fishing, and they know how to adapt to weather and topographical variations. Learn from their experience.

(BSL4) BASS LURES - TRICKS & TECHNIQUES - When bass become accustomed to the same artificials and presentations seen over and over again, they become harder to catch. You will learn how to modify your lures and rigs and how to develop new presentation and retrieve methods to spark the interest of largemouth!

(BSL5) SHALLOW WATER BASS - Bass spend 90% of their time in waters less than 15 feet deep. Learn productive new tactics that you can apply in marshes, estuaries, reservoirs, lakes, creeks and small ponds, and you'll triple your results!

> ### HAVE THEM ALL!
> *"Larry, I'm ordering one book to give a friend for his birthday and your two new ones. I have all the BASS SERIES LIBRARY except one, otherwise I would have ordered an autographed set. I have followed your writings for years and consider them the best of the best!"*
> J. Vinson, Cataula, GA

(BSL6) BASS FISHING FACTS - Learn why and how bass behave during pre- and post-spawn, how they utilize their senses when active and how they respond to their environment, and you'll increase your bass angling success!

(BSL7) TROPHY BASS - If you're more interested in wrestling with one or two monster largemouth than with a "panful" of yearlings, then learn what techniques and locations will improve your chances.

(BSL8) ANGLER'S GUIDE TO BASS PATTERNS - Catch bass every time out by learning how to develop a productive pattern quickly and effectively. "Bass Patterns" is a reference source for all anglers, regardless of where they live or their skill level. Learn how to choose the right lure, presentation and habitat under various weather and environmental conditions!

> ### TWO TROPHIES!
> *"By using your techniques and reading your Bass Series Library of books, I was able to catch the two biggest bass I've ever caught!"*
> B. Conley, Cromwell, IN

(BSL9) BASS GUIDE TIPS - Learn secret techniques known only in a certain region or state that often work in waters all around the country. It's this new approach that usually results in excellent bass angling success. Learn how to apply what the country's top guides know!

Nine Great Volumes To Help You Catch More and Larger Bass!

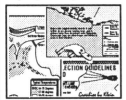

OUTDOOR TRAVEL SERIES
by Larry Larsen and M. Timothy O'Keefe

Candid guides on the best charters, time of the year, and other recommendations that can make your next fishing and/or diving trip much more enjoyable.

(OT1) FISH & DIVE THE CARIBBEAN -
Vol. 1 Northern Caribbean, including Cozumel, Cayman Islands, Bahamas, Jamaica, Virgin Islands. Required reading for fishing and diving enthusiasts who want to know the most cost-effective means to enjoy these and other Caribbean islands.

(OT3) FISH & DIVE FLORIDA & The Keys - Where and how to plan a vacation to America's most popular fishing and diving destination. Features include artificial reef loran numbers; freshwater springs/caves; coral reefs/barrier islands;

> **BEST BOOK CONTENT!**
> *"Fish & Dive the Caribbean" was a finalist in the Best Book Content Category of the National Association of Independent Publishers (NAIP). Over 500 books were submitted by publishers including Simon & Schuster and Turner Publishing. Said the judges "An excellent source book with invaluable instructions. Written by two nationally-known experts who, indeed, know what vacationing can be!"*

gulf stream/passes; inshore flats/channels; and back country estuaries.

DIVING SERIES by M. Timothy O'Keefe

(DL1) DIVING TO ADVENTURE shows how to get started in underwater photography, how to use current to your advantage, how to avoid seasickness, how to dive safely after dark, and how to plan a dive vacation, including live-aboard diving.

(DL2) MANATEES - OUR VANISHING MERMAIDS is an in-depth overview of nature's strangest-looking, gentlest animals. They're among America's most endangered mammals. The book covers where to see manatees while diving, why they may be living fossils, their unique life cycle, and much more.

UNCLE HOMER'S OUTDOOR CHUCKLE BOOK
by Homer Circle, Fishing Editor, Sports Afield

(OC1) In his inimitable humorous style, "Uncle Homer" relates jokes, tales, personal anecdotes and experiences covering several decades in the outdoors. These stories, memories and moments will bring grins, chuckles and deep down belly laughs as you wend your way through the folksy copy and cartoons. If you appreciate the lighter side of life, this book is a must!

OUTDOOR ADVENTURE LIBRARY
by Vin T. Sparano, Editor-in-Chief, Outdoor Life

(OA1) HUNTING DANGEROUS GAME - Live the adventure of hunting those dangerous animals that hunt back! Track a rogue elephant, survive a grizzly attack, and face a charging Cape buffalo. These classic tales will make you very nervous next time you're in the woods!

> **KEEP ME UPDATED!**
> *"I would like to get on your mailing list. I really enjoy your books!"*
> G. Granger, Cypress, CA

(OA2) GAME BIRDS & GUN DOGS - A unique collection of tales about hunters, their dogs and the upland game and waterfowl they hunt. You will read about good gun dogs and heart-breaking dogs, but never about bad dogs, because there's no such animal.

COASTAL FISHING GUIDES
by Frank Sargeant

A unique "where-to" series of detailed secret spots for Florida's finest saltwater fishing. These guide books describe hundreds of little-known honeyholes and exactly how to fish them. Prime seasons, baits and lures, marinas and dozens of detailed maps of the prime spots are included. The comprehensive index helps the reader to further pinpoint productive areas and tactics. Over $160 worth of personally-marked NOAA charts in the two books.

(FG1) FRANK SARGEANT'S SECRET SPOTS Tampa Bay to Cedar Key
Covers Hillsborough River and Davis Island through the Manatee River, Mullet Key and the Suwannee River.

(FG2) FRANK SARGEANT'S SECRET SPOTS Southwest Florida
Covers from Sarasota Bay to Marco.

INSHORE SERIES
by Frank Sargeant

(IL1) THE SNOOK BOOK-"Must" reading for anyone who loves the pursuit of this unique sub-tropic species. Every aspect of how you can find and catch big snook is covered, in all seasons and all waters where snook are found.

(IL2) THE REDFISH BOOK-Packed with expertise from the nation's leading redfish anglers and guides, this book covers every aspect of finding and fooling giant reds. You'll learn secret techniques revealed for the first time. After reading this informative book, you'll catch more redfish on your next trip!

(IL3) THE TARPON BOOK-Find and catch the wily "silver king" along the Gulf Coast, north through the mid-Atlantic, and south along Central and South American coastlines. Numerous experts share their most productive techniques.

(IL4) THE TROUT BOOK-Jammed with tips from the nation's leading trout guides and light tackle anglers. For both the old salt and the rank amateur who pursue the spotted weakfish, or seatrout, throughout the coastal waters of the Gulf and Atlantic.

HUNTING LIBRARY
by John E. Phillips

(DH1) MASTERS' SECRETS OF DEER HUNTING - Increase your deer hunting success by learning from the masters of the sport. New information on tactics and strategies is included in this book, the most comprehensive of its kind.

(DH2) THE SCIENCE OF DEER HUNTING Covers why, where and when a deer moves and deer behavior. Find the answers to many of the toughest deer hunting problems a sportsman ever encounters!

(DH3) MASTERS' SECRETS OF BOW-HUNTING DEER - Learn the skills required to take more bucks with a bow, even during gun season. A must read for those who walk into the woods with a strong bow and a swift shaft.

(TH1) MASTERS' SECRETS OF TURKEY HUNTING - Masters of the sport have solved some of the most difficult problems you can encounter while hunting wily longbeards with bows, blackpowder guns and shotguns. Learn the 10 deadly sins of turkey hunting.

> ### RECOMMENDATION!
> *"Masters' Secrets of Turkey Hunting is one of the best books around. If you're looking for a good turkey book, buy it!"*
> J. Spencer, Stuttgart Daily Leader, AR
>
> ### NO BRAGGIN'!
> *"From anyone else Masters' Secrets of Deer Hunting would be bragging and unbelievable. But not with John Phillips, he's paid his dues!"* F. Snare, Brookville Star, OH

(BP1) BLACKPOWDER HUNTING SECRETS - Learn how to take more game during and after the season with black powder guns. If you've been hunting with black powder for years, this book will teach you better tactics to use throughout the year.

FISHING LIBRARY

(CF1) MASTERS' SECRETS OF CRAPPIE FISHING by John E. Phillips Learn how to make crappie start biting again once they have stopped, select the best jig color, find crappie in a cold front, through the ice, or in 100-degree heat. Unusual, productive crappie fishing techniques are included.

(CF2) CRAPPIE TACTICS by Larry Larsen - Whether you are a beginner or a seasoned crappie fisherman, this book will improve your catch! The book includes some basics for fun fishing, advanced techniques for year 'round crappie and tournament preparation.

> ### CRAPPIE COUP!
> *"After reading your crappie book, I'm ready to overthrow the 'crappie king' at my lakeside housing development!"*
> R. Knorr, Haines City, FL

(CF3) MASTERS' SECRETS OF CATFISHING by John E. Phillips is your best guide to catching the best-tasting, elusive cats. If you want to know the best time of the year, the most productive places and which states to fish in your pursuit of Mr. Whiskers, then this book is for you. Special features include how to find and take monster cats, what baits to use and when, how to find a tailrace groove and more strategies for rivers or lakes.

LARSEN'S OUTDOOR PUBLISHING
CONVENIENT ORDER FORM
ALL PRICES INCLUDE POSTAGE/HANDLING

FRESH WATER
___ BSL1. Better Bass Angling Vol 1 ($11.95)
___ BSL2. Better Bass Angling Vol 2 ($11.95)
___ BSL3. Bass Pro Strategies ($11.95)
___ BSL4. Bass Lures/Techniques ($11.95)
___ BSL5. Shallow Water Bass ($11.95)
___ BSL6. Bass Fishing Facts ($11.95)
___ BSL7. Trophy Bass ($11.95)
___ BSL8. Bass Patterns ($11.95)
___ BSL9. Bass Guide Tips ($11.95)
___ CF1. Mstrs' Scrts/Crappie Fshng ($11.95)
___ CF2. Crappie Tactics ($11.95)
___ CF3. Mstr's Secrets of Catfishing ($11.95)
___ LB1. Larsen on Bass Tactics ($14.95)
___ PF1. Peacock Bass Explosions! ($14.95)

SALT WATER
___ IL1. The Snook Book ($11.95)
___ IL2. The Redfish Book ($11.95)
___ IL3. The Tarpon Book ($11.95)
___ IL4. The Trout Book ($11.95)

OTHER OUTDOORS BOOKS
___ DL1. Diving to Adventure ($11.95)
___ DL2. Manatees/Vanishing ($10.95)
___ OC1. Uncle Homer's Outdoor
Chuckle Book ($9.95)

REGIONAL
___ FG1. Secret Spots-Tampa Bay/
Cedar Key ($14.95)
___ FG2. Secret Spots - SW Florida ($14.95)
___ BW1. Guide/North Fl. Waters ($14.95)
___ BW2. Guide/Cntral Fl.Waters ($14.95)
___ BW3. Guide/South Fl.Waters ($14.95)
___ OT1. Fish/Dive - Caribbean ($13.95)
___ OT3. Fish/Dive Florida/ Keys ($13.95)

HUNTING
___ DH1. Mstrs' Secrets/ Deer Hunting ($11.95)
___ DH2. Science of Deer Hunting ($11.95)
___ DH3. Mstrs' Secrets/Bowhunting ($11.95)
___ TH1. Mstrs' Secrets/ Turkey Hunting ($11.95)
___ OA1. Hunting Dangerous Game! ($11.95)
___ OA2. Game Birds & Gun Dogs ($11.95)
___ BP1. Blackpowder Hunting Secrets ($13.95)

VIDEO &
SPECIAL DISCOUNT PACKAGES
___ V1 - Video - Advanced Bass Tactics $24.95
___ BSL - Bass Series Library (9 vol. set) $79.95
___ IL - Inshore Library (4 vol. set) $35.95
___ BW - Guides to Bass Waters (3 vols.) $37.95
Volume sets are autographed by each author.

BIG SAVINGS!
2-3 books, discount 10%
4 or more books, discount 20%

INTERNATIONAL ORDERS
Send check in U.S. funds; add
$2 more per book for airmail rate

ALL PRICES INCLUDE POSTAGE/HANDLING

No. of books ___ x $___ ea = $_____			*Special Package* ___ @ $_____		
No. of books ___ x $___ ea = $_____			*Special Package* ___ @ $_____		
No. of books ___ x $___ ea = $_____			*Video (50-min) $24.95 =* $_____		
SUBTOTAL $_____			*SUBTOTAL* $_____		

Multi-book Discount (%) $_____   *(N/A on discount packages or video)*

TOTAL ENCLOSED (check or money order)   **$_____**

*NAME*_____ *ADDRESS*_____

*CITY*_____ *STATE*_____ *ZIP*_____

Send check or Money Order to: Larsen's Outdoor Publishing, Dept. RD94
2640 Elizabeth Place, Lakeland, FL 33813 (813) 644-3381

Save Money On Your Next Outdoor Book!

Because you've purchased a Larsen's Outdoor Publishing Book, you can be placed on our growing list of **preferred customers.**

You can receive special discounts on our wide selection of Outdoor Libraries and Series, written by our expert authors.

PLUS...

Receive Substantial Discounts for Multiple Book Purchases

AND...

Advance notices on upcoming books and videos!

Yes, put my name on your mailing list to receive

1. Advance notice on upcoming outdoor books/videos
2. Special discount offers

Name_____

Address_____

City, State, Zip_____

Copy this page and send to: Larsen's Outdoor Publishing, 2640 Elizabeth Place, Lakeland, FL 33813